OECD Studies on Water

Towards Water Security in Belarus

A SYNTHESIS REPORT

OECD

BETTER POLICIES FOR BETTER LIVES

This work is published under the responsibility of the Secretary-General of the OECD. The opinions expressed and arguments employed herein do not necessarily reflect the official views of OECD member countries.

This document, as well as any data and map included herein, are without prejudice to the status of or sovereignty over any territory, to the delimitation of international frontiers and boundaries and to the name of any territory, city or area.

Please cite this publication as:
OECD (2020), *Towards Water Security in Belarus: A Synthesis Report*, OECD Studies on Water, OECD Publishing, Paris, *https://doi.org/10.1787/488183c4-en*.

ISBN 978-92-64-58396-2 (print)
ISBN 978-92-64-83130-8 (pdf)

OECD Studies on Water
ISSN 2224-5073 (print)
ISSN 2224-5081 (online)

Foreword

This publication provides the results of collaboration on water security between the Republic of Belarus (hereafter "Belarus"), the OECD and its partners implementing the EU-funded *EU Water Initiative Plus* project. As such, it is the most recent chapter in the OECD's long history of engagement on water-related issues in the region of Eastern Europe, the Caucasus and Central Asia (EECCA). The OECD has supported the EECCA countries since the early 1990s as they transitioned towards market economies following the disintegration of the Soviet Union. The OECD has provided guidance and expertise on strengthening water management as a major aspect of building greener economies and safeguarding long-term water, food and energy security. Its work has helped improve environmental and water management policies and facilitated the integration of environmental considerations into broader reform agendas.

However, OECD engagement on water-related topics in Belarus began later than in most other countries in the region. National Policy Dialogues (NPDs) on water, an important component of the OECD's efforts to support reform, began in most EECCA countries between 2006 and 2013,[1] whereas Belarus's journey towards launching an NPD began in 2018. Despite a slightly later start, the OECD's collaboration with Belarus has proven particularly productive in recent years. It has generated in-depth analysis on a wide range of topics related to water resource management and water security.

The European Union Water Initiative Plus for the Eastern Partnership (EUWI+), which began in 2016, has provided the impetus for closer collaboration with Belarus. The project was designed to support water resource management reform in all six Eastern Partnership (EaP) countries: Armenia, Azerbaijan, Belarus, Georgia, Moldova and Ukraine. The EUWI+ includes the OECD along with the UN Economic Commission for Europe (UNECE), the International Office for Water (IOWater) and the Austrian Environmental Agency (UBA) as implementing partners. The OECD and UNECE have been strategic partners for many years facilitating water NPDs in the EaP and wider EECCA region. However, EUWI+ presented an opportunity to work closely with a consortium of EU member states. This has provided a number of benefits for the project architecture, notably the blending of national-level policy reform recommendations with practical application of EU expertise in water management.

The EUWI+ aims to harmonise EaP country legislation with EU Water Framework Directive and other water-related directives in several ways. First, it will strengthen legislation, policy development and institutions. Second, it will modernise laboratory and monitoring systems. Third, it will help develop and implement river basin management plans (RBMPs). Fourth, it will improve data and information management on water resource management. The EUWI+ also aims to strengthen local capacity and improve communications, not least with civil society.

This publication clearly reflects these objectives, drawing upon the results of recent work with Belarus on water security issues on various levels. These include the national level (e.g. *Strategy of Water Resource Management in the Context of Climate Change for the Period until 2030*, which establishes water security as the country's main overarching policy objective), the subnational level (e.g. case studies in subnational jurisdictions such as Kopyl *rayon* of Minks *oblast* and several *rayon*s of Gomel *oblast*) and the transnational

---

[1] Armenia and Moldova in 2006, Ukraine in 2007 (relaunched in 2017 under EUWI+), Kyrgyzstan in 2008, Tajikistan in 2009, Azerbaijan and Turkmenistan in 2010, Georgia in 2011 and Kazakhstan in 2013.

level (in transboundary river basins). This publication synthesises the work from all EUWI+ implementing partners and outlines opportunities for future collaboration.

The Eastern Partnership region is bound together by its many transboundary water courses, and also by its shared inheritance of Soviet-era infrastructure and governance systems. While the region faces considerable risks to the quality and quantity of its water sources, these commonalities offer opportunities for policy exchange and peer learning. As such, the findings here provide lessons applicable beyond Belarus's borders, including but not limited to the other countries of the EaP region.

Chapter 1 situates this publication in the context of Belarus's overarching policy objective to ensure water security and briefly outlines the main results of EUWI+ work in this domain. As all readers may not be familiar with Belarus, **Chapter 2** provides an overview of the composition and distribution of the country's water resources, including the particular challenges facing different regions (*oblast*s) of Belarus. **Chapter 3** lays out the policy responses to the problems identified in Chapter 2 within the context of Belarus's new *Strategy of Water Resource Management in the Context of Climate Change for the Period until 2030.* **Chapter 4** concludes with an assessment of potential ways to boost water security in Belarus by supporting the country's ongoing reform agenda.

The OECD Environment Directorate prepared this report in co-operation with UBA, IOWater and UNECE – its EUWI+ implementing partners. The lead author was Douglas Herrick under the guidance of Matthew Griffiths and Alexandre Martoussevitch (all from the OECD Environment Directorate). Other contributing authors included Alexander Belokurov, Alisher Mamadzhanov and Nataliya Nikiforova (all UNECE), Paul Haener and Philippe Séguin (IOWater) and Alexander Zinke (UBA). The authors benefited from the comments of Snezhana Dubianok, Vladimir Korneev and Aleksandr Stankevich (Central Research Institute for Complex Use of Water Resources of the Republic of Belarus). Mark Foss edited the report and Lupita Johanson prepared it for publication.

This document was produced with the financial assistance of the European Union. The views expressed herein can in no way be taken to reflect the official opinion of the European Union.

This document and any map included herein are without prejudice to the status of, or sovereignty over, any territory, to the delimitation of international frontiers and boundaries, and to the name of any territory, city or area.

Table of contents

TABLES

Acronyms and local terms

Belstat: National Statistics Committee of Belarus

CRICUWR: Central Research Institute for Complex Use of Water Resources

EaP: Eastern Partnership

EECCA: Eastern Europe, the Caucasus and Central Asia

EU: European Union

EUWI: European Union Water Initiative

EUWI+: European Union Water Initiative Plus for the Eastern Partnership

GIS: Geographic Information System

HEPP: hydroelectric power plant

IOWater / OIEau: International Office for Water (*Office international de l'eau*)

IWRM: integrated water resources management

lcd: litres per capita per day *oblast*: region, first-level administrative division

rayon: district, second-level administrative division

RBMP: river basin management plan

RCAC: Republican Centre for Analytical Control in the Area of Environmental Protection

SDGs: Sustainable Development Goals

SEA: strategic environmental assessment

SEIS: Shared Environmental Information System

UBA: Environmental Agency of Austria (*Umweltsbundesamt*)

UNECE: United Nations Economic Commission for Europe

WFD: Water Framework Directive

WSS: water supply and sanitation

Executive Summary

The Republic of Belarus has established water security as the country's main overarching policy objective in the field of water resource management, notably in its draft *Strategy of Water Resource Management in the Context of Climate Change for the Period until 2030* (Water Strategy 2030). The strategy's primary focus is to achieve Sustainable Development Goal (SDG) 6, and Belarus plans to do so through six areas of reform. First, Belarus aims to introduce best available techniques and further improve water use efficiency. Second, it will better account for the impacts of climate change on water resources and adapt its water sector to climate change. Third, Belarus aims to improve surface and ground water monitoring systems. Fourth, it plans to introduce an integrated system of permits for nature users and reform its pricing system for water resources. Fifth, Belarus will adopt and implement river basin management plans, and lastly it will continue co-operation with its neighbours on transboundary rivers.

Under the European Union-funded project EU Water Initiative Plus (EUWI+), the OECD and the other implementing partners (Environment Agency of Austria, UBA; the International Office for Water of France, IOW; and the United Nations Economic Commission for Europe, UNECE) have actively supported Belarus's reform efforts towards achieving its water policy goals and its approximation of international legislation and good practice. EUWI+ has supported the implementation of the principles of the EU Water Framework Directive and of Integrated Water Resources Management, as well as Belarus's progress towards its international commitments.

The present publication compiles the results of Belarus's efforts since 2016 leading to greater levels of water security, including with support from EUWI+. For context, it provides an overview of the current state of water resources in Belarus in terms of quantity, distribution, quality, use and the challenges for current and future exploitation. It presents case studies on different regions of Belarus and their respective problems, including the comparatively water-rich Vitebsk *oblast* (region); the city of Minsk, which faces water stress due to demographic pressures; Gomel *oblast*, where water stress is of a seasonal nature; and rural areas like Kopyl *rayon* (district). Drawing on EUWI+ analysis, the publication identifies tools and techniques designed to respond to Belarus's regional needs and improve water security at both the local and national levels.

Key messages

- The country's water resources, though relatively abundant in per capita terms, are not evenly distributed across the country's six *oblast*s and are vulnerable to climatic impacts and threats from human activities. The effects of climate change include significant shifts in terms of the quantity and seasonality of water volumes in Belarus's river basins, and further changes are predicted. Other anthropogenic changes, both historic (e.g. the drying of wetlands due to Soviet-era irrigation works) and ongoing (e.g. wastewater discharges from households and industry, agricultural pollution), have significant impacts on water quality and availability.

- The overall population of Belarus is declining while urban centres, particularly Minsk, are growing. This trend, combined with the infrastructural heritage of the Soviet Union, has led to oversized centralised domestic water supply systems that operate at only a third of their installed capacity. Despite an overall excess of capacity, only 65.9% of rural inhabitants have access to centralised water supply systems and only 37.9% have access to centralised sanitation systems. As a result, many rural communities rely on shallow dug wells for water supply, with insufficient water quality monitoring, increasing risks to human health from water quality issues related to pollutants from agricultural runoff and other sources.

- Access to accurate, reliable datasets is a prerequisite for effective water resource management. Through its national statistics and monitoring systems (including on ground and surface water and on SDG 6.1-6.5 indicators), Belarus collects, manages and processes relevant datasets. The involvement of many different institutions in this domain necessitates good inter-institutional co-operation on data management to support decision making. The principles of the European Union funded Shared Environmental Information System (SEIS) provide a good framework for Belarus's continued reforms to improve its data management.

- Belarus has made considerable progress in adopting sound basin management in line with integrated water resources management principles, notably through the adoption of two river basin management plans and the creation of three basin councils. Under Water Strategy 2030, Belarus plans to establish two more basin councils by 2024, which would ensure coverage of all five of the country's transboundary river basins.

- Further improving water-use efficiency is a key component of Belarus's plans to bolster water security. Belarus's economy has become significantly less water-intensive over the past few decades. In 1990 52.1 m^3 of water was needed per USD 1 000 of GDP, whereas by 2018 the same output was achieved with only 7.3 m^3 of water. Focusing on four most water-intensive enterprises in the predominantly rural Kopyl *rayon*, EUWI+ helped develop new technological norms for industries on sustainable water use and wastewater discharge.

- Given the transboundary nature of the vast majority of its watercourses, Belarus attaches considerable importance to enhancing transboundary water co-operation with neighbouring states. EUWI+ has facilitated dialogues between Belarus, Latvia and Lithuania on shared transboundary river basins, and an intergovernmental agreement between Belarus and Poland on transboundary water protection was signed in 2020.

- Belarus has implemented an ambitious raft of reforms to its water management system, but areas for improvement remain. Through the implementation of Water Strategy 2030, Belarus aims to improve existing economic instruments and subsidies and introduce new instruments for water management, including discharge fees based on pollutant load. Belarus should also continue its efforts to ensure equitable access to water supply and sanitation, particularly in rural areas, and to progress towards meeting its international obligations (e.g. water-related Sustainable Development Goals, transboundary co-operation under the UNECE Water Convention and the UNECE-WHO/Europe Protocol on Water and Health). Belarus should continue developing and implementing river basin management plans, placing particular emphasis on high-quality data collection and management, local action as well as transboundary co-operation.

1 Towards water security in Belarus – an overview of the progress achieved through the European Union Water Initiative Plus Project

This chapter briefly presents the context of Belarus's water policy with its overarching objective to ensure water security. It outlines the work of the European Union Water Initiative Plus (EUWI+), which strives to support the harmonisation of Eastern Partnership (EaP) water resource management policies with the EU's Water Framework Directive and integrated water resource management principles, including through the facilitation of policy dialogues on water. It highlights the efforts designed to improve strategic and mid-term planning at the national, basin and local levels. Other EUWI+ activities covered in this chapter aim to strengthen co-operation on transboundary bodies of water, improve data management and the national monitoring framework, build local capacity and execute pilot projects to enhance water security.

The Republic of Belarus (hereafter "Belarus") has embarked on a series of reforms in the water sector to achieve the Sustainable Development Goals (SDGs) and transition towards a green economy model. Belarus has no formal obligation to implement the provisions of the Water Framework Directive (WFD) of the European Union (EU). Nevertheless, it has voluntarily committed to harmonising its water legislation and water management practices with those of the EU. The *Water Strategy of the Republic of Belarus for the period up to 2020* (Water Strategy 2020) established this reform process as a priority. To that end, the country's 2014 Water Code called for the development of river basin management plans (RBMPs), including for the Dnieper and Pripyat river basin districts. Belarus's national water policy objectives align with those of the EU Water Initiative Plus for the Eastern Partnership (EUWI+) project. This aims to support Eastern Partnership (EaP) countries[1] in bringing their national policies and strategies in line with the EU WFD (Box 1.1), integrated water resources management principles and commitments under relevant multilateral environmental agreements.

Box 1.1. EU Water Framework Directive

The EU Water Framework Directive (WFD), adopted in October 2000, is acknowledged as a model for water legislation and water policies. It provides a framework for water reform policies in EU member states and beyond.

In response to concerns by European citizens, the European Commission aims to get polluted waters clean again. In achieving these objectives, the role of citizens and citizens' groups is crucial. Specifically, the WFD's water protection goal aims at the following:

- Expanding the scope of water protection to all waters, including surface waters and groundwater.
- Achieving "good status" for all waters by a set deadline: a number of objectives define whether the quality of water is protected. All these objectives must be observed for each river basin and converge towards the "good status" of all water bodies.
- Managing water based on river basins: the natural geographical and hydrological unit is considered the best model for a single system of water management.
- Proposing a "combined approach" of emission limit values and quality standards.
- Getting the prices right: adequate water pricing acts as an incentive for the sustainable use of water resources and thus helps to achieve the environmental objectives under the directive.
- Getting citizens involved more closely: there are two main reasons for an extension of public participation. First, decisions on the most appropriate measures to achieve river basin management plan objectives will involve balancing the interests of various groups. Second, the implementation of decisions is likely to be more effective and lasting if endorsed by the public.
- Streamlining legislation: the framework directive approach streamlines the community's water legislation by replacing seven pieces of legislation, which can be repealed.

Source: European Commission (2019[1]), "Introduction to the EU Water Framework Directive", https://ec.europa.eu/environment/water/water-framework/info/intro_en.htm

---

Since 2016, the implementing partners of EUWI+[2] have actively supported Belarus's reform efforts. These include implementation of a national work programme under EUWI+, which was developed and agreed upon with Belarus, the European Commission and the implementing partners following a six-month, in-depth inception phase. For example, the country's new draft water strategy, Strategy of Water Resource Management in the Context of Climate Change for the Period until 2030 (hereafter "Water Strategy 2030"), was drafted with the support of EUWI+. It is designed to align with relevant national documents, including the Water Code and the National Strategy for Sustainable Socio-Economic Development to 2030. It also is intended to meet international commitments such as the SDGs, the UN Economic Commission for

Europe (UNECE) Water Convention, the UNECE-World Health Organization (WHO) Regional Office for Europe Protocol on Water and Health (hereafter "the Protocol on Water and Health"), and bilateral agreements on transboundary water bodies.

It defines achieving long-term water security as its main strategic goal and sets up specific strategic targets formulated in terms of SDG 6 actions.

1.1. Policy dialogue on water and sustainability

When the EUWI+ started, Belarus lacked a platform for a multi-stakeholder policy dialogue on water that brought together actors from different sections and levels of the water governance system. With the support of EUWI+, Belarus created an inter-agency committee in 2018, which serves as a steering body for EUWI+ project implementation in the country. At the same time, the committee is a platform for policy dialogue on water management issues involving key stakeholders from various levels of the water governance system. This has included identification and commissioning of cross-sectoral pilot projects, including a study on water management in irrigation in the water-stressed south of the country.

1.2. Strategic and mid-term planning at the national, basin and local levels

Belarus has pursued various paths for strategic and mid-term planning. EUWI+ supported the preparation of Water Strategy 2030 and helped carry out a strategic environmental assessment (SEA) of the draft; adoption of the strategy was expected by the end of February 2021. Several studies under EUWI+ informed the development of the future national water supply and sanitation (WSS) strategy. These focused on improving potable water supply in rural settlements, and on options for improving sludge treatment. Drafting for the WSS strategy began in the second half of 2020. In addition, a study on environmental tax aims to help improve use of policy instruments for implementing strategic and mid-term plans in the water sector. Finally, activities took place to build local capacity regarding economic instruments for managing water resources, bodies and systems (Section 3.2.1).

The project also supported the development of river basin management plans (RBMPs) for the Dnieper and Pripyat river basins (covering the parts of the basin located within the territory of Belarus – see Box 1.2)[3]. The Dnieper RBMP was approved on 31 December 2019, while the draft Pripyat RBMP was to have firstly pass through public hearings: they were part of the second meeting of the Pripyat river basin council held in October 2020. After that, the official approval of the Pripyat RBMP is expected before the completion of EUWI+ in February 2021.

Box 1.2. River basin management planning

Rivers provide a multitude of services such as water supply; waste assimilation; fisheries; energy production; flood attenuation; spiritual, cultural and recreational benefits; and the habitat that supports a wide range of ecosystems. Consequently, planning for their use is complex. The demands on rivers increasingly exceed their natural capabilities, resulting in over-abstraction, pollution, infestation of alien species, floodplain alteration and habitat destruction. These failures are usually the result of poor decision making, inadequate management and inappropriate planning. To minimise these consequences, effective basin planning is the starting point for sustainable management of river basins.

Many international actors have converged towards the principle of managing water at a basin scale because this approach opens up several environmental and economic opportunities. The OECD's Council Recommendation on Water, adopted in December 2016, states that water policies should be set up and implemented based on long-term water management plans, preferably at the river basin or aquifer level. Other organisations, including the Global Water Partnership, the International Network of Basin Organizations and UNESCO, have produced guidelines for water management in basins. These typically divide the role of basin institutions into three main functions:

1. monitoring, investigating, co-ordinating and regulating
2. planning and financing
3. developing and managing.

More importantly, these guidelines advise river basin organisations to look at the "big picture". These organisations should aim to become the leading voice on basin-wide issues. At the same time, they should keep constituencies and decision makers in all sectors and at all levels, in both the public and private sectors, fully informed and involved. In particular, UNESCO's guidelines form part of a series of documentation on strategic water management and include recommendations on basin water allocation planning.

River basin management planning, a requirement of the European Union Water Framework Directive, is a holistic and integrated approach to water resource management and aquatic ecosystems. It is used to improve human health and the quality of water resources and ecosystems, as well as foster economic development and consistency between sectoral policies. The output is a non-technical, clear planning document: the river basin management plan (RBMP). These are developed with an established methodology and public participation to enhance awareness and inform decision makers. Box 3.2 describes the development process of the document in accordance with Annex VII of the EU's Water Framework Directive. RBMPs typically contain successive chapters describing characterisation of the river basin (drivers, pressures, status, impacts); diagnosis and main issues; trends and objectives; programme of measures and dashboard.

Sources: OECD (2016[2]), *OECD Council Recommendation on Water*, OECD, Paris, https://www.oecd.org/environment/resources/Council-Recommendation-on-water.pdf; OECD (2015[3]), *Water Resources Governance in Brazil*, OECD Publishing, Paris, http://dx.doi.org/10.1787/9789264238121-en.

During 2020, Belarus aims to adopt a national action plan to implement water, sanitation, hygiene and health targets set under the Protocol on Water and Health. Setting national targets under the Protocol on Water and Health is a legal requirement for all Parties to the Protocol; Belarus has been an active Party since 2009. With support from EUWI+, the country was revising initial targets set in 2013. It aimed to align the targets with the objectives and principles of the 2030 Agenda for Sustainable Development and with relevant areas of the EU water policy. These areas included prevention, safety, risk-based management, equity of access and attention to hygiene.

The EUWI+ project also supported mid-term planning at the local level in a pilot *rayon* (district, a second-order subnational unit). Kopyl *rayon* in Minsk *oblast* (region) was selected. Belarus elaborated recommendations on developing potable water supply systems in rural settlements as a substantive input to the future mid-term *rayon*-level master plan for WSS. Finally, an OECD-led study examined options for resuming irrigation in pilot *rayon*s of Gomel *oblast* (in Pripyat river basin) where the impact of climate change on water resources is most visible.

1.3. Strengthening co-operation on transboundary bodies of water

Strong transboundary co-operation is a key water policy objective of Belarus, which shares river basins with a number of EU member states, EaP countries and the Russian Federation (hereafter "Russia"). EUWI+ supported the work of intergovernmental bodies and their working groups on the upper Dnieper and Pripyat rivers. It also ensured inputs from Belarus to working groups under the UNECE Convention on the Protection and Use of Transboundary Watercourses and International Lakes.

With support of the European Union under EUWI+, UNECE also facilitated the participation of Belarusian delegations in negotiations on transboundary rivers and expert work with neighbouring Latvia and Lithuania. In addition, under the project, Belarus received methodological support and capacity development under the Water Convention and reporting on SDG indicator 6.5.2 on transboundary water co-operation, in 2018 and 2020.

1.4. Strengthening the national monitoring framework and improving data management for informed decision making in the water sector

The water-related SDGs, enshrined in the draft Water Strategy 2030, require the nationalisation of indicators and the establishment of a corresponding monitoring network to track implementation. To address these demands, with EUWI+ support Belarus developed methodologies to calculate and monitor SDG 6.3-6.5 and integrated them into the State Water Cadastre. This allowed for the automated production of time series at different levels of data aggregation (by basins and territorial-administrative units, by main economic sectors), and facilitated the exchange of data on respective SDG indicators with all interested bodies. The National Statistics Committee of Belarus (hereafter "Belstat") endorsed the indicators and the methodologies, which were then approved by the Ministry of Natural Resources and Environment in November 2019. In parallel, EUWI+ provided support to strengthening local capacity for national reporting on indicator SDG 6.5.2.

Before EUWI+, Belarus had well-established surface water and groundwater monitoring systems compared to other EaP countries.[4] Still, they fell short of WFD standards. Belarus needed to improve the capacity of data management, laboratory equipment and staff to carry out hydrochemical, hydrobiological and hydromorphological monitoring in the field and in the laboratory. In response, the EUWI+ project developed laboratory staff capacity and procured a range of modern laboratory equipment.[5] By the end of the project, laboratory equipment was to be installed and fully operational, and laboratory staff trained in its use and in overall quality management. This effort was expected to significantly increase confidence in the country's analytical data, bringing them in line with good EU practice and WFD requirements.

To build on investments in the production of high quality analytical data, Belarus sought to improve the management of water data. The aim was to achieve maximum transparency and value of data collected to inform decision making. The EUWI+ project mapped all relevant actors in data management and intended to support the purchase of a data server. This would set the stage for a platform for multi-stakeholder data exchanges. This platform would ensure access to available datasets produced and managed by national organisations. Belarus would need a national data management strategy to ensure appropriate governance and confidence around the data hosted.

1.5. Pilot actions to enhance water security at the local level

It will be challenging for Belarus to prioritise and manage implementation of Water Strategy 2030, the RBMPs, the Protocol on Water and Health, the WSS strategy and associated mid-term plans and programmes of measures. To assist in this process, under EUWI+ several pilot actions were supported.

The pilot work in Kopyl *rayon* (district) of the Minsk oblast (province) was aimed to develop a comprehensive solution for sustainable water use at local level. In this predominantly rural subdivision of the Minsk *oblast,* the local government has welcomed in-depth analytical work to tackle water management challenges. The work included new water use and water discharge norms in water-intensive industries, as well as recommendations for a future master plan on potable water supply in rural settlements. Successful pilot activities in Kopyl could be considered for wider roll out in other *rayon*s of Belarus.

Sub-basin management plans, such as those supported through the Dnieper RBMP (covering the Uza river and a number of small water courses in Mogilev city), could also help solve local issues as part of the broader basin-level planning process.

1.6. Local capacity development

During its six-month inception phase, EUWI+ identified the need to develop local capacity in a number of areas. These included strategic planning and the application of economic instruments in water resource management and reporting under SDG 6.5.2. At the river-basin level, EUWI+ has strengthened experts' capacity through workshops and surveys for planning, monitoring, data management and public consultation.

To develop local expert capacity in using economic instruments for water resource management, EUWI+ helped develop training materials that use examples from both Belarus, the EU and other countries in the region of Eastern Europe, the Caucasus and Central Asia. Interested national universities have already started using these materials to support training of future water economists and specialists in developing and implementing water policy.

EUWI+ also helped build capacity in SEA after it became mandatory in 2017. Specifically, it helped deliver a SEA of the draft Water Strategy 2030. National experts took part in two training sessions in July 2019 and March 2020 in Minsk to deepen their knowledge about SEA process and techniques and to prepare reports.

The impact of capacity development efforts on surface and groundwater body delineations, RBMPs and field surveys (biology, chemistry, hydromorphology), as well as enhanced laboratory analysis, is discussed in Section 2.3.

Notes

[1] The Eastern Partnership is a joint initiative launched at the Prague Summit in May 2009 that aims to deepen and strengthen economic and strategic relations between the EU and six of its eastern neighbours: Armenia, Azerbaijan, Belarus, Georgia, Moldova and Ukraine.

[2] EUWI+'s implementing partners are the Environment Agency of Austria (UBA, *Umweltbundesamt*), the International Office for Water of France (OIEau, *Office international de l'eau*), the OECD and UNECE.

[3] In the Republic of Belarus, the Dnieper RBMP covers the area of the Dnieper River Basin inside the country without its main tributary Pripyat, which is covered by its own RBMP. The confluence of the Pripyat and Dnieper rivers is located in Ukraine.

[4] Specifically, the Republican Centre for Analytical Control in the field of Environmental Protection (RCAC) in Minsk was accredited according to the international standard EN ISO/IEC 17025.

[5] The Minsk RCAC received a liquid chromatography-mass spectrometry and mass spectrometry equipment. This allowed the determination of additional WFD priority substances, such as perfluorinated compounds, pesticides and hexabromocyclododecane. The RCAC in Gomel received an atomic fluorescence spectrometer to determine trace-level amounts of mercury in surface waters. In 2020, the Central Laboratory of the Research and Production Centre for Geology received consumables for operating the groundwater laboratory.

References

European Commission (2019), *Introduction to the EU Water Framework Directive*, http://ec.europa.eu/environment/water/water-framework/info/intro_en.htm. [1]

OECD (2016), *OECD Council Recommendation on Water*, OECD, Paris. [2]

OECD (2015), *Water Resources Governance in Brazil*, OECD Studies on Water, OECD Publishing, Paris, https://dx.doi.org/10.1787/9789264238121-en. [3]

2 State of play

This chapter provides an overview of the composition and distribution of the country's water resources across the river basins and regions (oblasts) of Belarus. It presents the effects of climate change and other anthropogenic pressures on the quantity, quality and seasonal availability of water resources as well as the progress Belarus has made over time towards a less water-intensive economy. It includes four case studies displaying the diversity of challenges facing different oblasts in Belarus with varying endowments of water resources and demographic trends and pressures. The chapter also describes the policy instruments and legal, regulatory and institutional frameworks that form the country's water resource management system. On the subject of monitoring surface and groundwater, the chapter presents concrete examples of how the process of delineating water bodies and monitoring water quality has taken place in Belarus through the European Union Water Initiative Plus project.

2.1. State of water resources in Belarus

The Republic of Belarus (hereafter "Belarus") straddles a watershed. Some of its river basins drain into the Baltic Sea to the north-northwest (e.g. West Dvina/Daugava, Neman and Western Bug river basins). Others flow to the Black Sea in the south-southeast (e.g. Dnieper and Pripyat river basins). About 55% of surface water runoff in Belarus drains into the Black Sea, while the remainder flows into the Baltic Sea.

A network of large and medium-sized rivers combined with some 10 000 lakes ensures that Belarus enjoys relatively high levels of fresh water availability. Out of 57.9 billion cubic metres (m^3) of water that flows through Belarus, 58% is formed locally (Minprirody, 2018[1]). On average, Belarus's large and medium-sized rivers carry about 57.9 cubic kilometres (km^3) of fresh water through the country. The flow can reach up to 92.4 km^3 and can drop as low as 37.2 km^3 (Deraviaha and Dubianok, 2020[2]).

Given the relative abundance of surface water runoff and the country's modestly sized population of 9.5 million, the per capita water availability in Belarus is 3 590 m^3/year (UNECE, 2016[3]). Belarus benefits from more water resources in per capita terms than its larger neighbours (Poland and Ukraine), but benefits from slightly less than smaller ones (Latvia and Lithuania) (Figure 2.1).

Figure 2.1. Per capita water resources are more abundant in Belarus than in its larger neighbours

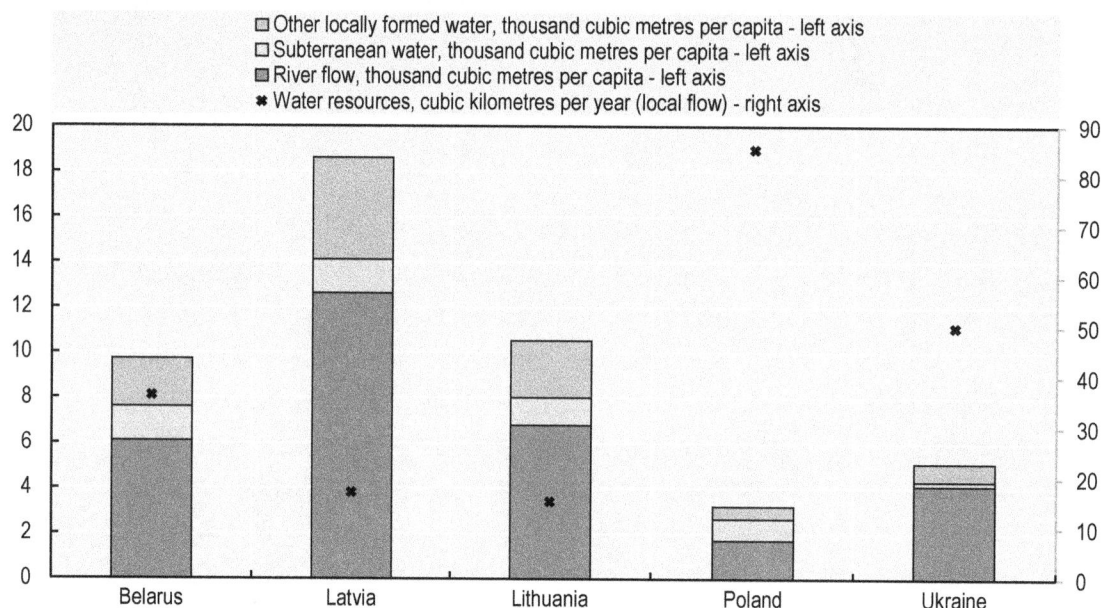

Source: Minprirody (2018[1]), «Стратегия управления водными ресурсами в условиях изменения климата на период до 2030 года (проект)» [The Strategy of Water Resource Management in the Context of Climate Change for the Period Until 2030: Draft], Central Research Institute for Complex Use of Water Resources, Ministry of Natural Resources and Environmental Protection of the Republic of Belarus.

The last large-scale evaluation of Belarus's confined groundwater resources took place in the early 1980s, but their actual capacity is estimated at 49.6 million m^3 per day. Much of this water naturally contains geogenic dissolved minerals, such as boron, iron, silica and hydrogen sulphide. It is already exploited for drinking water, bottled mineral water and curative bathing complexes (sanatoria) (Minprirody, 2018[1]). The *Strategy of Water Resources Management in the Context of Climate Change for the Period until 2030* recommended further study of particularities and potential uses of Belarus's groundwater resources.

Fresh groundwater in Belarus, as in many countries of Eastern Europe, often naturally contains high concentrations of iron. Other dissolved minerals typically found in relatively high concentrations in its groundwater include manganese, boron and fluorine. In the best-case scenario, fresh groundwater is unpalatable. In the worst-case scenario, it is unfit for human consumption without appropriate treatment.

Due to natural geogenic background conditions, iron levels exceed the maximum allowable concentration of 0.3 milligrams per litre (mg/L) in water from 70% of Belarus's boreholes nationwide, and from 90-95% in the southern border region of Polesia. Such sources require iron removal treatment facilities to satisfy guidelines for drinking water quality (Deraviaha and Dubianok, 2020[2]).

In addition to the dissolved minerals naturally occurring in most of the country's groundwater, shallow groundwater horizons also suffer from considerable anthropogenic pollution. This is predominantly caused by the storage and disposal of agricultural chemicals, from both diffuse and point sources. For these substances, prevention at the source is better than treatment at the tap. Belarus needs to strengthen monitoring to define the natural background concentrations and identify which groundwater and surface waters suffer from anthropogenic pollution. These data would help Belarus accurately account for both underlying geogenic conditions and pressures from human activity. This, in turn, would serve as a reliable way to verify information about its water resources and to set priorities for improving and maintaining water quality.

2.1.1. Anthropogenic and climatic impacts on Belarus's water resources

The country's water resources, though abundant, are not evenly distributed and are vulnerable to climatic impacts and threats from human activities. Its numerous springs, for example, play an essential role in maintaining the stability of hydrological systems. However, many were destroyed in the second half of the 20th century due to poorly planned and executed irrigation and construction projects (Minprirody, 2018[1]).

The average annual flow in most river basins in Belarus has increased. According to time series data between 1880 and 2015, 85% of the average flow of Belarusian rivers rose in the summer and autumn months. Average flow increased on 49% of the country's rivers in a statistically significant manner and more than doubled on 18% of rivers. The base flow decreased on 15% of rivers. However, the shifts were only statistically significant on the Sluch and Viliya rivers. The construction of the Soligorsk reservoir in 1967 and the Vileyka-Minsk water conveyance system in 1976 had dramatic impacts on the two rivers.

The increased flow recorded in the summer and autumn is believed to stem from drainage works. Whereas it previously accumulated in peat bogs and gradually evaporated, water now runs more quickly into drainage canals (Volchek et al., 2017[4]). Irrigation works throughout the 1960s, 1970s and 1980s led to the drying of 20 000 km² of wetlands (primarily peat bogs). This occurred particularly along the southern edge of the country in the Belarusian part of Polesia.

Due to the drying wetlands, an estimated 5.6 km³ of water was lost, leading to a decrease in groundwater levels reaching 1-1.5 m in the central and southern parts of Belarus (Deraviaha and Dubianok, 2020[2]). Total mineralisation of groundwater, including concentrations of sulphates, iron and calcium, increased over this period. Meanwhile, the concentration of organic substances decreased. Increased mineralisation also occurred in surface waters. This was compounded by the intensive use of fertilisers on the drained land, which increased the concentrations of nitrogen and phosphorous from runoff.

The country's water resources have shifted due to climate change over the past century, with seasonal phenomena changing significantly. The peak of the spring runoff, for instance, has occurred earlier in the year since the 1980s. It has shifted from the middle of March (in the southwest) and mid- to late April (in the northeast) to March throughout the entire country. Maximum flow rates of spring floods decreased noticeably between 1966-2005 compared to 1877-1965. Increasing average temperatures led to more thawing episodes over the winter, which led to reduced snow reserves by the end of the low-water winter season. As with all climate change-related shifts, the effect was not uniform throughout the country (see Section 2.2). Some *oblasts* such as Grodno, for example, were more impacted than others (e.g. Brest).

Overall, the maximum spring runoff decreased by 43% on average across the country between the two periods (Volchek et al., 2017[4]).

Flash floods, particularly in the summer and autumn when most crops are either growing or being harvested, are often more economically damaging than springtime thaw floods. Overall, the intensity of rainwater floods and the amplitude of their variation have decreased over time in most river basins. The most notable exception is the Pripyat river basin (Volchek et al., 2017[4]).

In winter, conversely, base flow increased on 90% of rivers in Belarus. In all, 53% experienced statistically significant changes and 20% of rivers more than doubled in flow volume. The increase in winter base-flow volumes, is linked primarily to climatic factors since higher average temperatures in winter lead to more regular thaws (Volchek et al., 2017[4]).

Human activity had and continues to have a considerable impact on water quality. The drainage of swampland led to an increase in groundwater's apparent colour due to contamination of water-soluble humic substances. Ammonium and nitrate compounds, which are by-products of peat mineralisation, have also seeped into groundwater. An estimated 1.5 million tonnes (t) of minerals and 700 000 t of water-soluble organic substances drain into the Black Sea via the Pripyat and Dnieper rivers running through dried wetlands (Deraviaha and Dubianok, 2020[2]).

Wastewater discharges from households and industry, as well as non-point sources such as runoff from urban and agricultural areas, also deteriorate water quality. Major sources of water pollution include leachate from municipal waste sites, sludge disposal, filtration fields and fertiliser storage. Equally important sources are untreated water discharges from livestock farms and flows of wastewater and storm water from major cities (e.g. runoff from Minsk into the Svisloch river). The wastewater treatment plants built in many medium and small cities in the 1970s and 1980s require modernisation or rehabilitation. They cannot meet the modern wastewater quality requirements of the EU's Urban Waste Water Treatment Directive, especially in terms of nitrogen and phosphorous concentrations (Deraviaha and Dubianok, 2020[2]).

Agricultural pollution, both diffuse and point source, can lead to excessive levels of nitrogen, phosphorous, potassium and sodium through runoff. This can find its way into rivers, watercourses and groundwater. In Belarus, some rural populations in small settlements rely on non-centralised water supply systems such as shallow wells without sufficient oversight of water quality. As a result, agriculture-linked nitrate pollution of drinking water supplies is a health risk. Tests have confirmed that nitrate levels occasionally exceed maximum acceptable concentrations several times over. Furthermore, water drawn from wells near agricultural areas often does not satisfy drinking water norms in terms of chemical content and microbiological indicators (Deraviaha and Dubianok, 2020[2]). Pesticides are also a freshwater quality issue in some areas (e.g. Minsk *oblast*).

Belarus's water resources are valuable not only for human use, but also for their role in supporting biodiversity and precious ecosystems. Belarus is home to swamps, lake complexes and other bodies of water that support fragile ecosystems that are relatively rare in Europe. Populations of wetland flora and fauna have decreased due to climate change-linked pressures. These have been compounded by other anthropogenic factors, including habitat fragmentation and degradation (UNECE, 2016[3]).

2.1.2. Water use in Belarus

The primary challenge for ensuring water security is balancing economic needs and environmental considerations for water use. Worldwide, the biggest issues include the lack of fresh water compared to present or projected needs and the inefficient use of water for irrigation in agriculture. In addition, many regions – including the EU due to its high concentration of industrial activity – face a further challenge: the need to reduce the negative impacts of industrial wastewater discharges on the environment. Belarus has high levels of per capita water availability compared to the worldwide average and less intensive industrial activity compared to the EU. Its greatest challenge is improving the effective use of water by end-users, particularly households and water-intensive industries such as food processing (Deraviaha and Dubianok, 2020[2]).

Agriculture accounts for a smaller share of Belarus's water use (36%) than the global average (69%), but more than in Europe on average (25%) (Figure 2.2). While industry uses a larger share of water in Belarus (25%) than elsewhere in the world (19%), in Europe industry uses more than twice as much (54%). In Belarus, households use the most water (39%), accounting for a much larger share of water use than the European and global averages (21% and 12%, respectively).

Belarus's water resources offer untapped potential on several levels. The proposed 33 megawatt (MW) Beshenkovichi hydroelectric power station on the Daugava/West Dvina river, for example, could develop renewable energies. Inland water transport and lakeside and river tourism and recreation are other examples. In Belarus, the potential exploitable flow for hydroelectricity power generation – particularly prevalent in the Neman, West Dvina/Daugava and Dnieper river basins – could reach 850 MW, with 520 MW technically available, and 250 MW – economically feasible (Deraviaha and Dubianok, 2020[2]).

Figure 2.2. Water use by sector in Belarus, Europe and the world

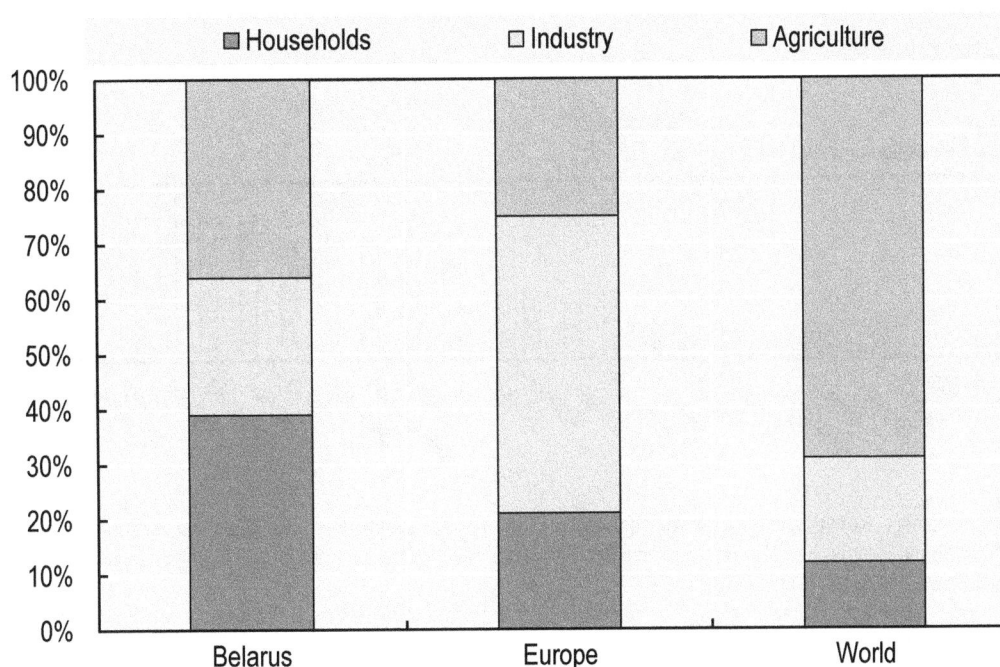

Source: Deraviaha, I. & S. Dubianok (2020[2]), «Экономические инструменты управления водными ресурсами и объектами и водохозяйственными системами в Республике Беларусь: тематические материалы проекта «Водная инициатива ЕС плюс для Восточного партнерства»» [Economic Instruments for the Management of Water Resources, Bodies of Water and Water Systems in the Republic of Belarus: Thematic Materials under the EU Water Initiative Plus for the Eastern Partnership], Belarusian State Technological University.

Although households are the largest end-users of Belarus's water, it has a significantly oversized centralised domestic water supply system given the country's population. It has installed capacity sufficient to deliver 4.3 million m³ of water per day. However, it operates at just over a third of this capacity, supplying 1.6 million m³ per day on average. The system consists of 10 197 boreholes, 598 iron removal stations and 38 200 km of distribution network. Much of this system contributes to poor tap water quality due to the level of physical deterioration (Deraviaha and Dubianok, 2020[2]).

Despite an overall national overcapacity of centralised water supply system, many small settlements are not connected to centralised drinking water supply systems.

Overall, relative to the country's vast renewable fresh water resources and compared to other European countries, annual water usage rates are low in Belarus. Freshwater withdrawals amount to only 4.8% of total available freshwater resources, far below the 25% threshold defining initial water stress (Figure 2.3). Water abstractions in 2016 were 1 405 million m^3. Of this amount, 365 million m^3 was from surface water sources and 819 million m^3 was from subterranean sources (Minprirody, 2018[1]).

Figure 2.3. Belarus is among those European countries below the threshold of initial water stress

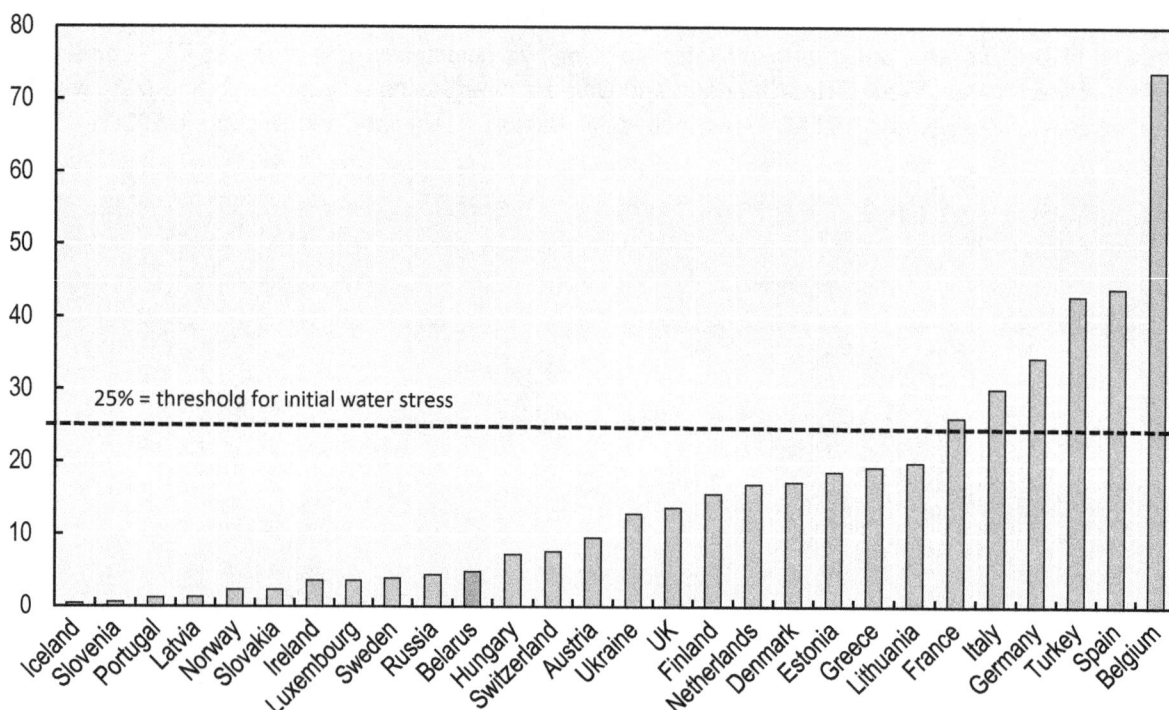

Note: Data for Finland, Greece, Norway and Portugal from 2005; for Austria, Belgium, Denmark, France, Germany, Ireland, Sweden, Switzerland and the UK from 2010; for Belarus, Estonia, Hungary, Iceland, Italy, Latvia, Lithuania, Luxembourg, the Netherlands, Russian Federation, Slovakia, Slovenia, Spain, Turkey and Ukraine from 2015.
Source: FAO (n.d.[5]), "Sustainable Development Goals: Indicator 6.4.2 – Level of water stress: Freshwater withdrawal as a proportion of available freshwater resources", webpage, www.fao.org/sustainable-development-goals/indicators/642/en/

Belarus, like many countries in Eastern Europe[1], is experiencing a gradual decrease in its population. Its national water usage rates follow a similar downward trend (Figure 2.4). In particular, as shown Figure 2.4(b), water use for domestic needs has declined over the past two decades, while the amount of water used for other purposes has remained more stable. Figure 2.4(a) shows that population decline is primarily in rural areas (particularly outside the Minsk region), whereas urban areas have grown slightly (particularly in the city of Minsk itself). If these trends continue, water usage rates could continue to decline in Belarus overall, and particularly in rural areas in peripheral regions. At the same time, Minsk and other growing urban areas may add stress to local water resources.

As shown in Figure 2.4(b), households account for the largest share of Belarus's water use, followed by industry and agriculture, where pond fish farming uses several times more water than the rest of agriculture. In 2014, however, fishing and fish farming represented only a small share of the country's GDP (approximately 0.1%), while agriculture represented 7.7% of GDP (UNITER, 2016[6]). Examples of particularly water-intensive industries in Belarus include cellulose and paper products, petroleum refining and plastics production, and food processing industry (CRICUWR, 2019[7]).

Figure 2.4. Population and water use have both gradually decreased over the past two decades

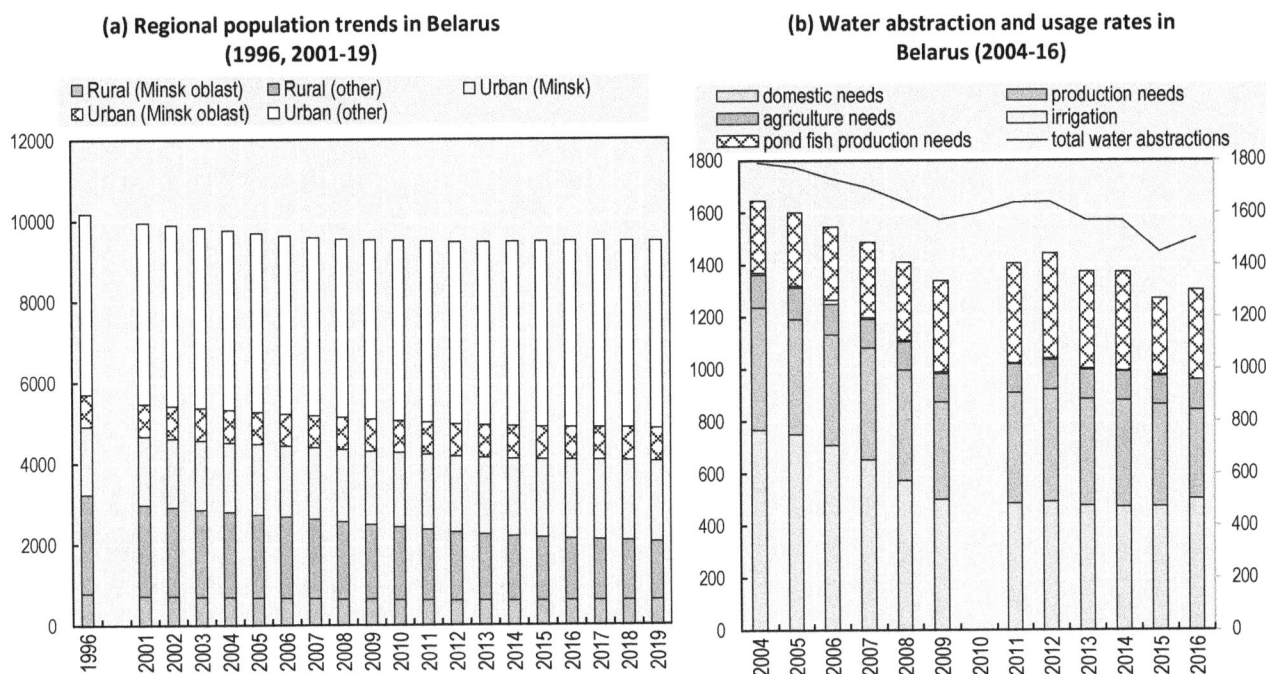

(a) Regional population trends in Belarus (1996, 2001-19)

☐ Rural (Minsk oblast) ☐ Rural (other) ☐ Urban (Minsk)
☒ Urban (Minsk oblast) ☐ Urban (other)

(b) Water abstraction and usage rates in Belarus (2004-16)

☐ domestic needs ☐ production needs
☐ agriculture needs ☐ irrigation
☒ pond fish production needs — total water abstractions

Note: (a) Population numbers from the beginning of each calendar year; (b) no data on sectoral use for 2010; "irrigation" refers to irrigated agriculture and "agriculture needs" refers to other water uses for agriculture.
Source: (a) Belstat (2019[8]), «*Численность населения по областям и г. Минску*» [Population by Region and in the City of Minsk], National Statistical Committee of the Republic of Belarus, www.belstat.gov.by/ofitsialnaya-statistika/solialnaya-sfera/naselenie-i-migratsiya/naselenie/godovye-dannye/; (b) CRICUWR (2018[11]), «Стратегия управления водными ресурсами в условиях изменения климата на период до 2030 года (проект)» [The Strategy of Water Resource Management in the Context of Climate Change for the Period Until 2030: Draft], Central Research Institute for Complex Use of Water Resources, Ministry of Natural Resources and Environmental Protection of the Republic of Belarus; Minprirody (2011[9]), «Водная стратегия Республики Беларусь на период до 2020 года» [Water Strategy of the Republic of Belarus for the Period until 2020], Ministry of Natural Resources and Environmental Protection of the Republic of Belarus, www.minpriroda.gov.by/ru/new_url_1649710582-ru/.

While water usage rates have declined, Belarus's economy has continued to grow. This decoupling has contributed to the improved water efficiency of the economy, with smaller volumes of water required for each unit of output (Figure 2.5). While 52.1 m³ of water was needed per USD 1 000 of gross domestic product (GDP) in 1990, the same output was achieved with only 31.3 m³ of water in 2000 and 7.3 m³ of water in 2018. This dramatic increase in water efficiency was achieved due to several factors. Belarus introduced water-saving technologies. It also developed and implemented technological standards for water use by water-intensive enterprises. In addition, it increased water abstractions fees and water supply tariffs and introduced better water accounting measures in enterprises and households. As a result, the economy in Belarus is less water-intensive than other EaP countries and even some EU countries like Lithuania, Poland and France. However, it is slightly more water-intensive than Germany and Latvia (Figure 2.6).

Figure 2.5. Belarus's economy has become less water-intensive over time

Annual volume of abstracted freshwater (m³) per unit of GDP (USD 1 000, purchasing power parity in current international dollars) in 1990, 1995 and 2000-18

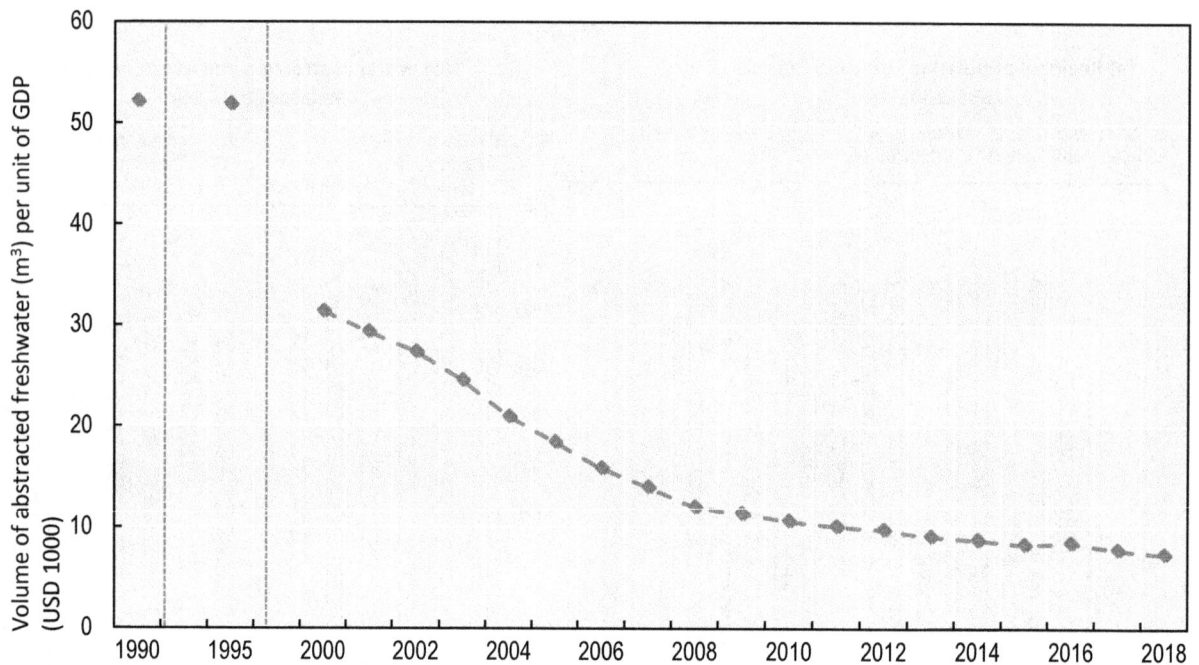

Note: GDP data in units of USD 1 000, purchasing power parity in current international dollars.
Source: Belstat (2019[10]), C.3. Водопотребление [C.3. Water Consumption] (database), National Statistical Committee of the Republic of Belarus, www.belstat.gov.by/ofitsialnaya-statistika/makroekonomika-i-okruzhayushchaya-sreda/okruzhayuschaya-sreda/sovmestnaya-sistema-ekologicheskoi-informatsii2/c-vodnye-resursy/c-3-vodopotreblenie/; World Bank (2020[11]), World Development Indicators (database), https://data.worldbank.org/.

Figure 2.6. Water intensity of Belarus, EaP countries and selected EU economies

Cubic metres (m³) of freshwater water abstractions per USD 1000, purchasing power parity (PPP) in current international dollars (all data from 2015, except Germany from 2016)

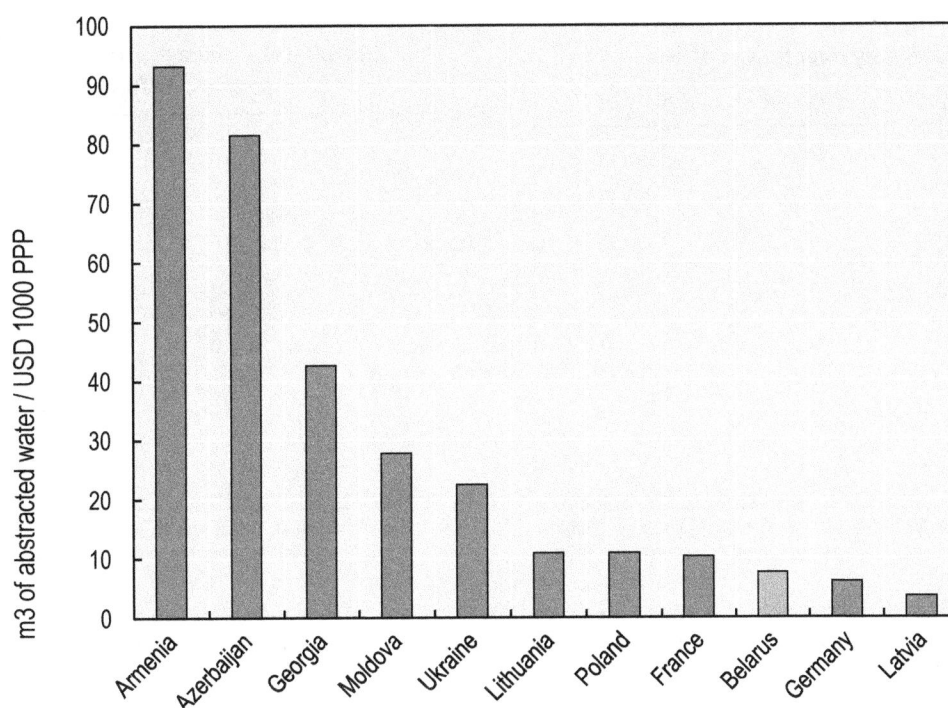

Note: GDP data in units of USD 1000, PPP in current international dollars. Ukraine data exclude the temporarily occupied territory of the Autonomous Republic of Crimea, the city of Sevastopol and a part of temporarily occupied territories in the Donetsk and Luhansk regions. *Source:* Statistical Committee of the Republic of Armenia (2020[12]), « Water Abstraction, mln. m³ / 2020 », *Time Series* (database), www.armstat.am/en/?nid=12&id=14004&submit=Search; State Statistical Committee of the Republic of Azerbaijan (2020[13]), 9.1. Su ehtiyatlarının mühafizəsini və onlardan istifadə edilməsini səciyyələndirən əsas göstəricilər [*[9.1. Key Indicators Characterising the Protection and Use of Water Resources]* (database), www.stat.gov.az/source/environment/az/009_1.xls; Belstat (2019[10]), C.3. Водопотребление [C.3. Water Consumption] (database), National Statistical Committee of the Republic of Belarus, www.belstat.gov.by/ofitsialnaya-statistika/makroekonomika-i-okruzhayushchaya-sreda/okruzhayuschaya-sreda/sovmestnaya-sistema-ekologicheskoi-informatsii2/c-vodnye-resursy/c-3-vodopotreblenie/; European Environment Agency (2018[14]), "C2 – Freshwater Abstraction in Georgia", *ENI SEIS II East* (database), https://eni-seis.eionet.europa.eu/east/indicators/c2-2013-freshwater-abstraction-in-georgia; Statistica Moldovei (2019[15]), "The Main Indicators of Water Use, 2001-2018", *Water Use* (database), http://statbank.statistica.md/PxWeb/pxweb/en/10%20Mediul%20inconjurator/10%20Mediul%20inconjurator__MED020/MED020100.px/; Ukrstat (2018[16]), *Main Indicators on the Water Resources Use and Protection* (database), https://ukrstat.org/en/operativ/operativ2006/ns_rik/ns_e/opvvr_rik_e2005.htm; Eurostat (2020[17]), Fresh water abstraction by source - million m³ (database), https://ec.europa.eu/eurostat/databrowser/view/ten00002/default/table?lang=en; World Bank (2020[11]), *World Development Indicators* (database), https://data.worldbank.org/.

2.2. Regional distribution of water resources and the level of development of water infrastructure systems in Belarus

Belarus's six administrative regions, known as *oblast*s (*voblast* in Belarusian), and their 118 subdivisions, known as *rayon*s, differ widely in terms of their water resources (Figure 2.7). The country's population and economy are concentrated in the central region, Minsk *oblast*. However, this *oblast* benefits from less surface water (7.6 km³/year on average) than surrounding regions and especially the eastern *oblast*s of Mogilev (14.6 km³/year), Vitebsk (18.1 km³/year) and Gomel (31.5 km³/year). Water resources in Gomel *oblast* are also notable for the much wider variation between recorded high and low annual flows. In terms of groundwater, however, Minsk *oblast* has the most resources on average (10 700 m³/day) along with Vitebsk *oblast* (10 260 m³/day). Other *oblast*s have considerably less proven groundwater reserves.

Figure 2.7. Average water resources by administrative region

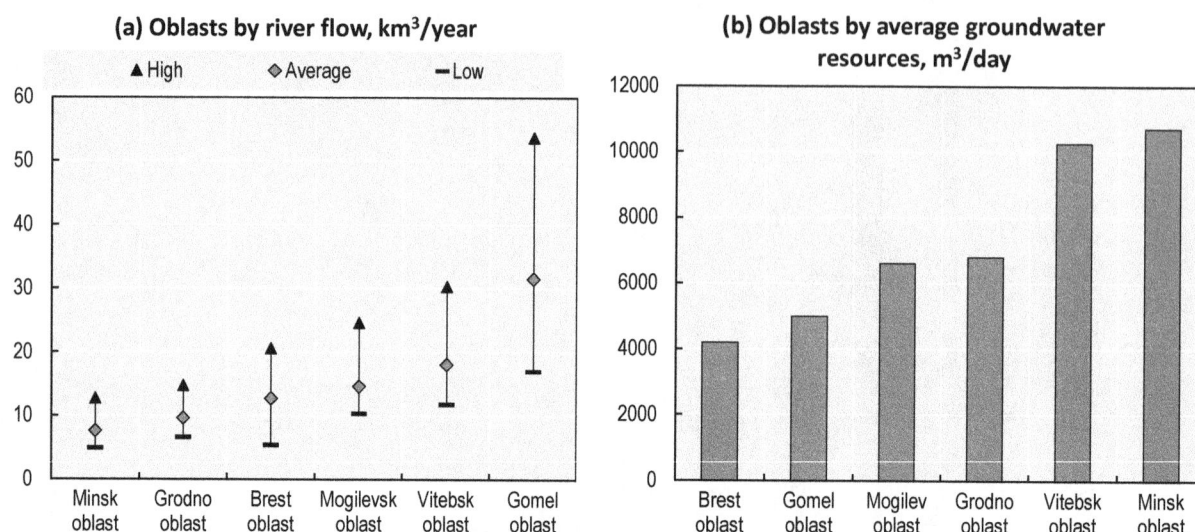

Source: CRICUWR (2019[7]), Водные ресурсы, их использование и качество вод (за 2018 год) [State Water Cadastre: Water Resources, their Use and Water Quality (in 2018)], Central Research Institute for Complex Use of Water Resources, Ministry of Natural Resources and Environmental Protection of the Republic of Belarus.

Five transboundary river basins cross parts of Belarus's territory (Figure 2.8).

Two drain into the Black Sea:

- the Dnieper river basin – in the east of Belarus, covering most of Mogilev region and portions of the Gomel, Vitebsk and Minsk *oblast*s
- the Pripyat river basin – in the south of Belarus, including parts of the Gomel, Minsk and Brest *oblast*s.

The remaining three drain into the Baltic Sea:

- the West Bug river basin – the southwest corner of the country, primarily in the Brest *oblast*
- the Neman river basin – in the west, mostly in the Grodno *oblast*, but also in the Minsk and Brest *oblast*s
- the West Dvina/Daugava river basin – in the north, primarily in the Vitebsk *oblast*.

Figure 2.8. River basin districts in Belarus

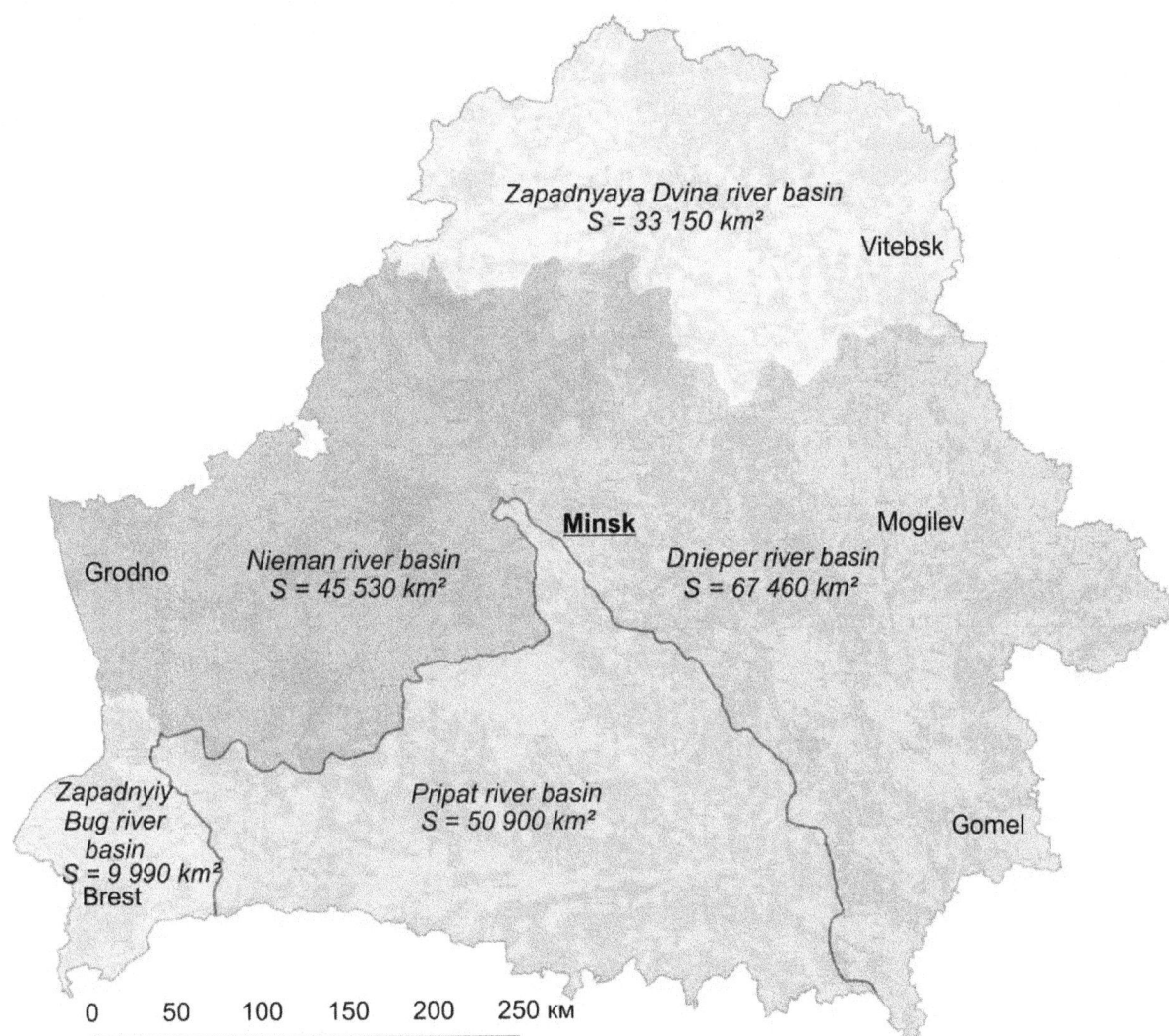

Source: CRICUWR.

The volumes flowing through Belarus's river basins have shifted over time. Specialists from the Central Research Institute for Complex Use of Water Resources (CRICUWR) and Brest State Technical University predict they will differ considerably in the future. Between 1961-1984 and 1985-2009, water volumes in the Dnieper and especially the West Dvina/Daugava river basins increased in the autumn and winter, and decreased in the spring and beginning of the summer, compared to the runoff profile in 1961–1984 (Figure 2.9a). The Neman and Pripyat river basins exhibited similar shifts in the first half of each calendar year, though in October-December the Pripyat's volumes decreased while the Neman basin maintained broadly stable volumes in the second half of the year (Volchek et al., 2017[4]).

Average annual volumes in the West Dvina/Daugava and Neman river basins (broadly corresponding to the northern and western parts of the country) are predicted to increase by 2035. Meanwhile, lower than average volumes are expected in the West Bug, Dnieper and especially the Pripyat river basins are expected (Figure 2.9b).

These diverging patterns are most evident in the summer. During those months, run-off in the West Dvina/Daugava river basin are expected to increase by 21% compared to current levels. Meanwhile, run-off in the West Bug and Pripyat river basins is expected to drop by 23% and 25%, respectively.

All river basins will have higher volumes in the winter months (Neman, +20%; West Dvina/Daugava, +11%; West Bug, +8%; Dnieper +4%) except the Pripyat river basin (-1%). In the spring and autumn, run-off in the West Dvina/Daugava and West Bug river basins will increase in volume, while in the Pripyat and the Dnieper run-off will decline. In the Neman river basin the run-off is projected to increase slightly in the summer months, but decrease in the autumn (Volchek et al., 2017[4]).

Sections 2.2.1-4 offer four brief profiles to illustrate the various challenges facing Belarus's *oblast*s. They will cover (1) Vitebsk *oblast*, a comparatively water-rich region; (2) Minsk city, facing water stress due to demographic pressures; (3) Gomel *oblast*, confronted with seasonal water stress; and (4) rural areas, exemplified by the Kopyl *rayon* in the Minsk *oblast*.

Figure 2.9. Observed and projected trends in seasonal water volumes by river basin

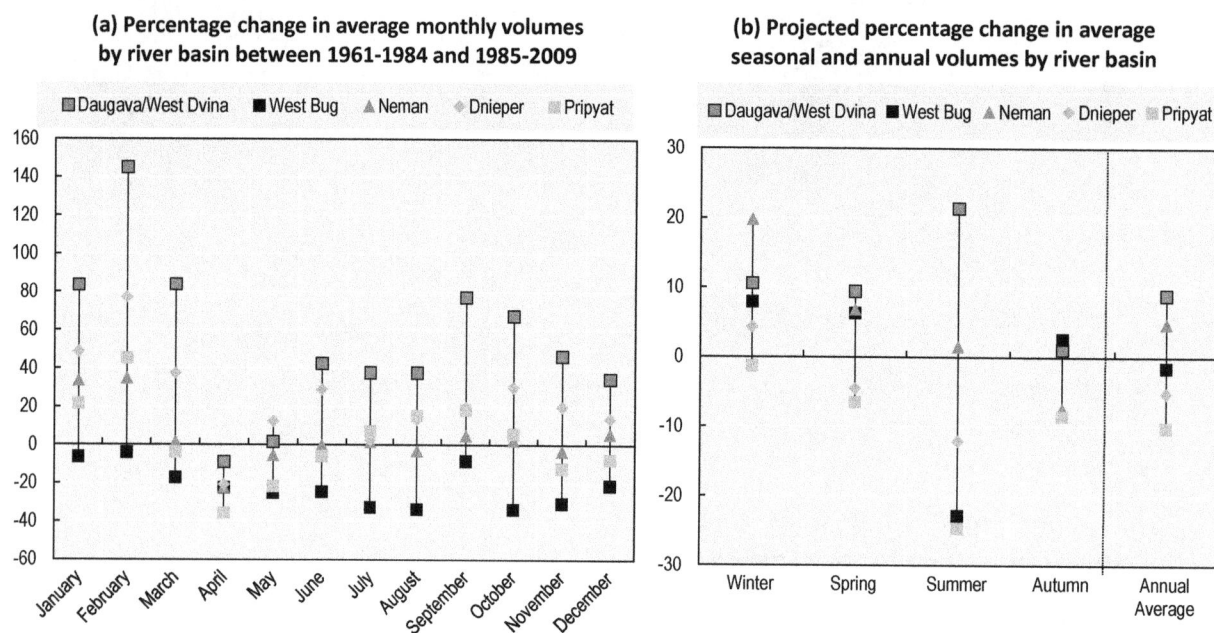

(a) Percentage change in average monthly volumes by river basin between 1961-1984 and 1985-2009

(b) Projected percentage change in average seasonal and annual volumes by river basin

Source: Volchek et al. (2017[4]), «Водные ресурсы Беларуси и их прогноз с учетом изменения климата» [Water Resources of Belarus and their Forecast Accounting for Climate Change], Central Research Institute for Complex Use of Water Resources, Ministry of Natural Resources and Environmental Protection of the Republic of Belarus, Alternativa, Brest.

2.2.1. Vitebsk oblast

The Vitebsk *oblast*, in northern Belarus, borders Lithuania to the west, Latvia to the northwest and the Russian Federation (hereafter "Russia") to the east and northeast. One of the most water-rich *oblast*s of the country, it lies almost entirely in the West Dvina/Daugava river basin. This basin has experienced, and is projected to continue to experience, increasing volumes of water (Deraviaha and Dubianok, 2020[2]; Volchek et al., 2017[4]). The West Dvina/Daugava river basin covers 87 900 km² of territory primarily in Belarus (38%), but also in Latvia (27%) and Russia (21%), as well as in Estonia and Lithuania (14%). Winter floods during 1988-2010 increased by 20-40% on the rivers of the West Dvina/Daugava river basin compared to 1966-1987. However, the magnitude of rainwater and springtime floods decreased between the two periods (Volchek et al., 2017[4]).

The West Dvina/Daugava river basin in Belarus experiences intensive water use by industrial, agricultural and energy facilities. The West Dvina/Daugava is one of the main navigable arteries of the country with a length of 108.9 km of waterways in service within the basin. The West Dvina/Daugava river in the Vitebsk *oblast* hosts two of the largest hydroelectric power plants (HEPPs) in Belarus: Vitebsk HEPP (40 MW) and Polotsk HEPP (21.7 MW). The two HEPPs jointly account for about two-thirds of the country's installed hydropower generation capacity of 95.8 MW. A third major power plant, the 33-MW Beshenkovichsky HEPP, was also planned in the Vitebsk portion of the West Dvina/Daugava basin (Minprirody, 2018[1]). The country's largest power station, the gas-fired Lukomlskaya State District Power Station, with 2 889.5-MW capacity, is located on the river's banks.

Lakes and wetlands are an integral part of the landscapes and the natural environment of the West Dvina/Daugava river basin. They play a key role in the regulation and formation of river flow and water self-purification. The global importance of the basin's wetland ecosystems derives from its unique biodiversity. The quality and quantity of the water resources of the West Dvina/Daugava river basin depend on effective water management in the drainage area. Effective water management, in turn, has large impacts on the ecological status of the Baltic Sea.

2.2.2. Minsk city

Unlike Vitebsk *oblast*, where total water withdrawals in 2018 only amounted to about 1% of the average annual volume of water in the region, the capital Minsk and the surrounding Minsk *oblast* have fewer resources and use them more intensively (Figure 2.10). Together, they abstracted 7% of the Minsk *oblast*'s average annual water resources, making it the most water-intensive *oblast* of Belarus relative to its resources by far. The city of Minsk, which is home to over 20% of Belarus's population and over 30% of the country's GDP, applies considerable pressure on the surrounding region's water resources: it has the second highest per capita daily water usage rate after Mogilev city (Figure 2.11). Since the city and region of Minsk are the only parts of Belarus that have enjoyed positive demographic growth over the past two decades (Belstat, 2019[18]), pressures on regional water resources will likely continue to grow.

While the rest of Belarus relies exclusively on groundwater resources for drinking water, the city of Minsk also draws from surface sources for its drinking water due to the density of water users. A major 62.5-km canal, the Vileysko-Minsk water system, was built in 1968-76. It brings water from the Viliya water reservoir (Neman river basin) to the Svisloch river (Dnieper river basin) for the growing capital city (Deraviaha and Dubianok, 2020[2]). As much as this canal may benefit local water supply security, mixing waters of the Baltic Sea and Black Sea basins may trigger the spread of invasive species. This, in turn, would alter water ecosystems and their economic use.

Figure 2.10. Freshwater withdrawal rates by *oblast* and as a percentage of average annual water resources

Freshwater withdrawals in 2018 (in million m^3) on the left axis and as a percentage of the average annual volume of water resources in the region on the right axis

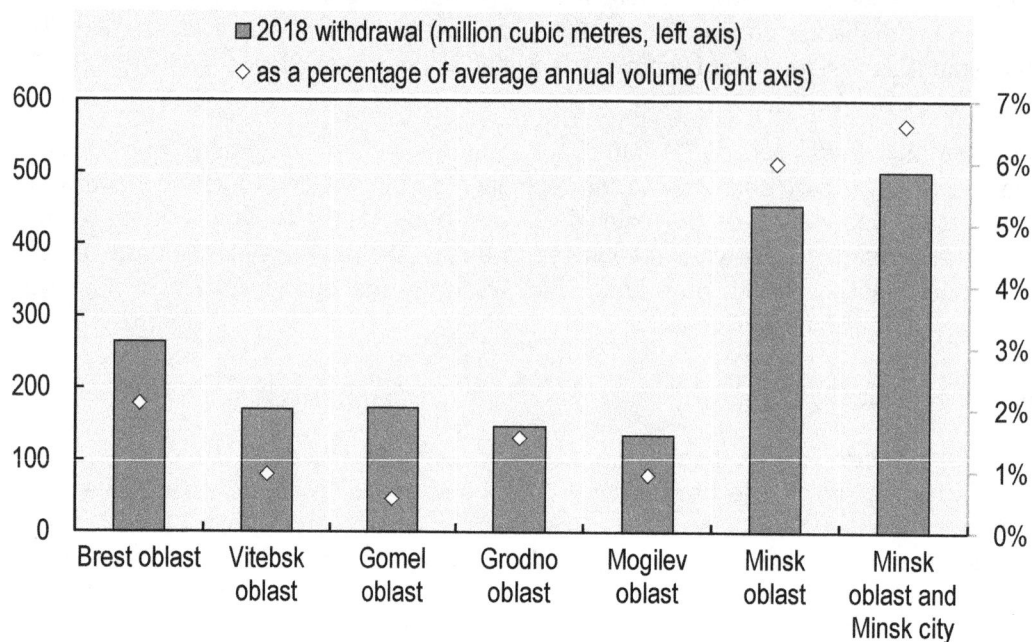

Note: No data for the average annual volume of water resources in Minsk city.

Source: CRICUWR (2019[7]), Государственный водный кадастр: Водные ресурсы, их использование и качество вод (за 2018 год) [State Water Cadastre: Water Resources, Their Use and Water Quality (in 2018)], Central Research Institute for Complex Use of Water Resources, Ministry of Natural Resources and Environmental Protection of the Republic of Belarus.

Figure 2.11. Daily per capita water usage rates by oblast and city (2017)

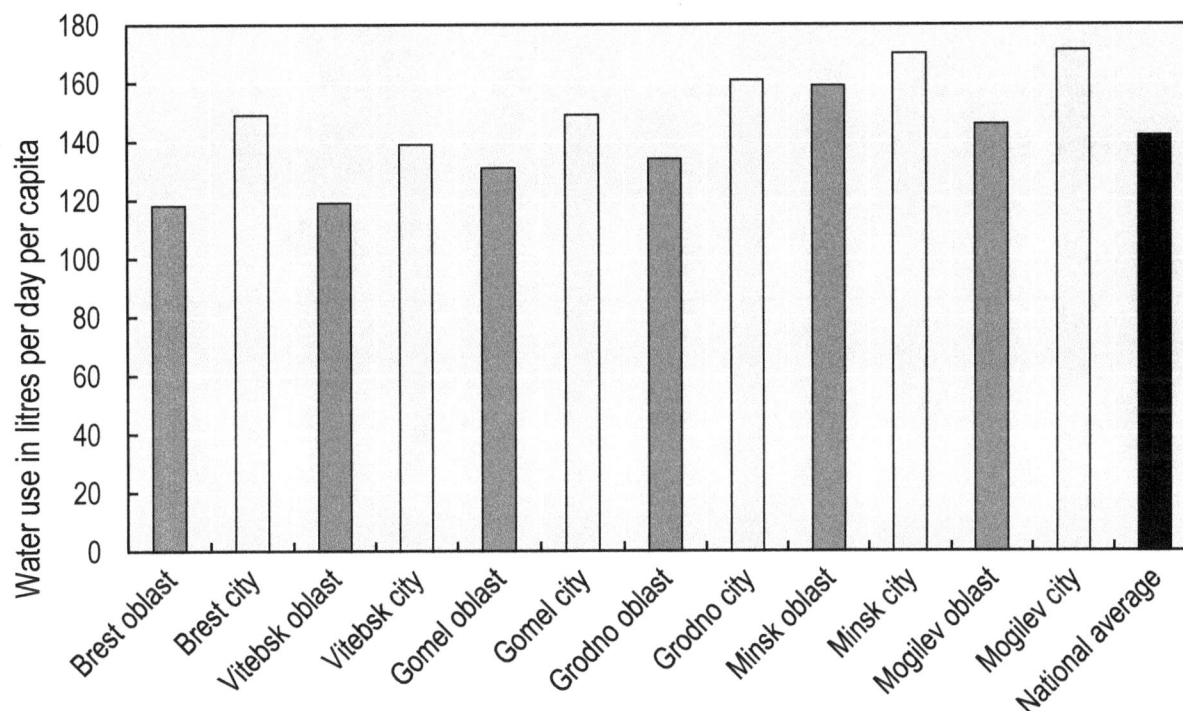

Source: Deraviaha, I. and S. Dubianok (2020[2]), «Экономические инструменты управления водными ресурсами и объектами и водохозяйственными системами в Республике Беларусь: тематические материалы проекта «Водная инициатива ЕС плюс для Восточного партнерства»» [Economic Instruments for the Management of Water Resources, Bodies of Water and Water Systems in the Republic of Belarus: Thematic Materials under the EU Water Initiative Plus for the Eastern Partnership], Belarusian State Technological University.

2.2.3. Gomel oblast

Some parts of the Gomel oblast face water shortages of a seasonal nature. Located in the southeast corner of Belarus, it borders Ukraine to the south and Russia to the east. Along with Brest oblast, Gomel is one of the oblasts with the least abundant ground water resources in Belarus. However, it is home to the most bountiful and yet most variable surface water resources in the country (CRICUWR, 2019[7]). The runoff in the vegetation period of the region's primary river, the Pripyat, is projected to decrease by up to 25% by 2035 compared to current levels. This is due, in part, to a climate change-linked reduction in precipitation. These projected trends could exacerbate the variable quantity of Gomel's surface water resources during a key period for its economy, given the importance of the agricultural sector in Gomel. Agriculture, forestry and commercial fishing and fish farming account for 12.2% of Gomel oblast's gross regional product. This makes it the second most agriculture-oriented region of Belarus after Brest (13.5% of its gross regional product) (Belstat, 2019[19]). Certain agricultural districts of the Gomel region have already reported that reduced runoff and precipitation rates have had an adverse effect on crop yields.

By the 1980s, irrigation systems were already well developed and operational; irrigated agriculture was a large water user. However, over the past three decades, the use of irrigation for agriculture has dropped dramatically (Figure 2.12). Consequently, the country's irrigation infrastructure has been neglected and fallen into disrepair. Given its seasonal water shortages, Gomel oblast could benefit from the rehabilitation of irrigation infrastructure to support water security and agricultural productivity. Alternatively, it could change land use away from agriculture or to less water-intensive crops in response to climate change's impact on water resources. An assessment of the economic feasibility and water security impacts and trade-offs of rehabilitating or adapting the region's irrigation infrastructure started under EUWI+ in May 2020.

Figure 2.12. Water use for irrigation in Belarus (1990-2015), by water supply source

in million m^3 per annum

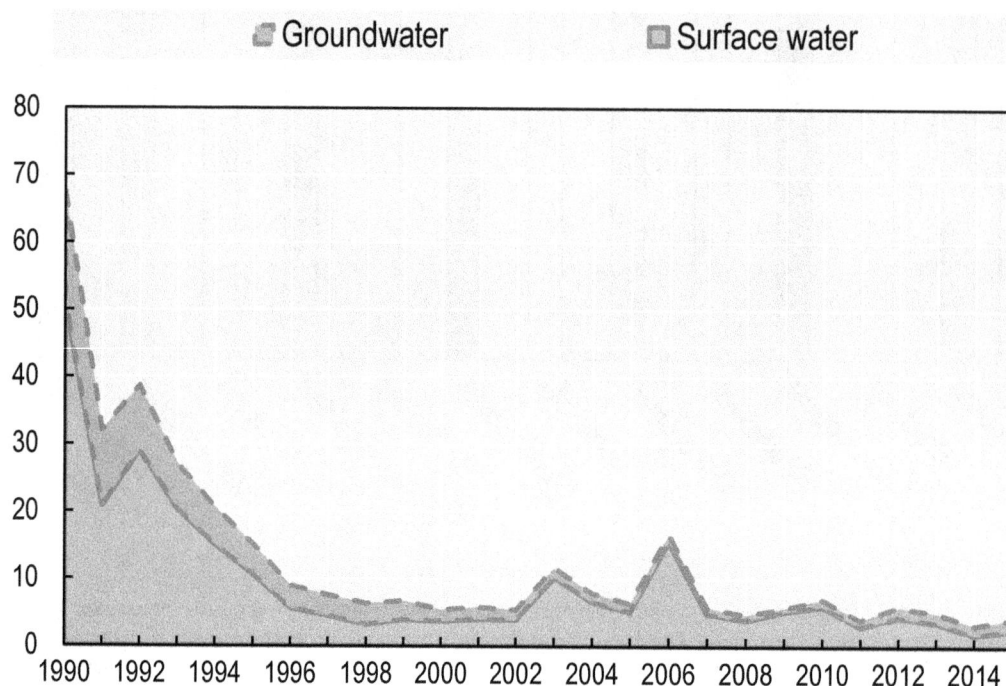

Source: CRICUWR.

2.2.4. Kopyl rayon, Minsk oblast

Belarus has achieved near-universal access to centralised water supply systems in its urban areas (98.5%) and to centralised sanitation (92.8%). However, the country's rural areas have considerably worse access to these services. Only 65.9% of rural inhabitants have access to centralised water systems, while only 37.9% are connected to centralised sanitation systems. Some 1.5 million Belarusians (over 15% of the population), primarily in rural areas, rely on non-centralised water sources such as shallow dug wells. These wells often do not benefit from regular maintenance, cleaning or water quality checks to ensure safety for human consumption (Minprirody, 2018[1]).

In this regard, the Kopyl *rayon* of the Minsk *oblast* exemplifies the country's urban-rural disparities. In the town of Kopyl, the *rayon*'s largest settlement, 98% of the population enjoys access to centralised water supply systems, while only 27% of the population of the *rayon*'s rural settlements has such access (Figure 2.13). Kopyl *rayon*, is home to several agricultural settlements ("agrotowns") with 70% access on average. Out of Kopyl *rayon*'s ten village councils, which are the *rayon*'s administrative subdivisions, only two village councils achieve over 50% access (Figure 2.14).

A peculiarity of centralised water supply systems in the Kopyl *rayon* is the involvement of non-traditional operators. Kopyl Housing and Municipal Utilities (*Копыльское ЖКХ*), a communal unitary enterprise, provides such services. In addition, agricultural firms and even state education facilities (schools) supply water to parts of Kopyl district's population (Section 3.2.2.1).

Figure 2.13. Percentage of the population connected to centralised water supply system in Kopyl rayon

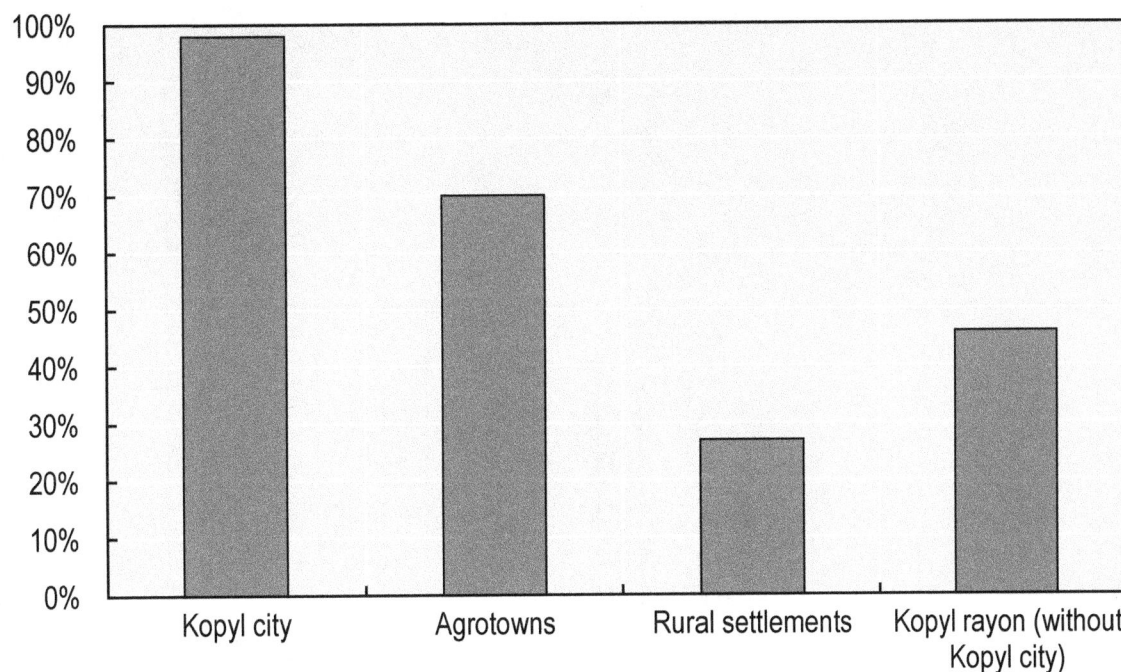

Source: CRICUWR (2019[20]), «Разработка рекомендаций по развитию систем хозяйственно-питьевого водоснабжения в Копыльском районе Минской области Беларуси» [Elaboration of Recommendations on the Development of Domestic Drinking Water Supply Systems in the Kopyl Rayon of the Minsk Oblast of Belarus], prepared by a team of experts led by P. Zakharko from the Central Research Institute for Complex Use of Water Resources, Ministry of Natural Resources and Environmental Protection of the Republic of Belarus.//

Figure 2.14. Proportion of population connected to centralised drinking water supply by village council

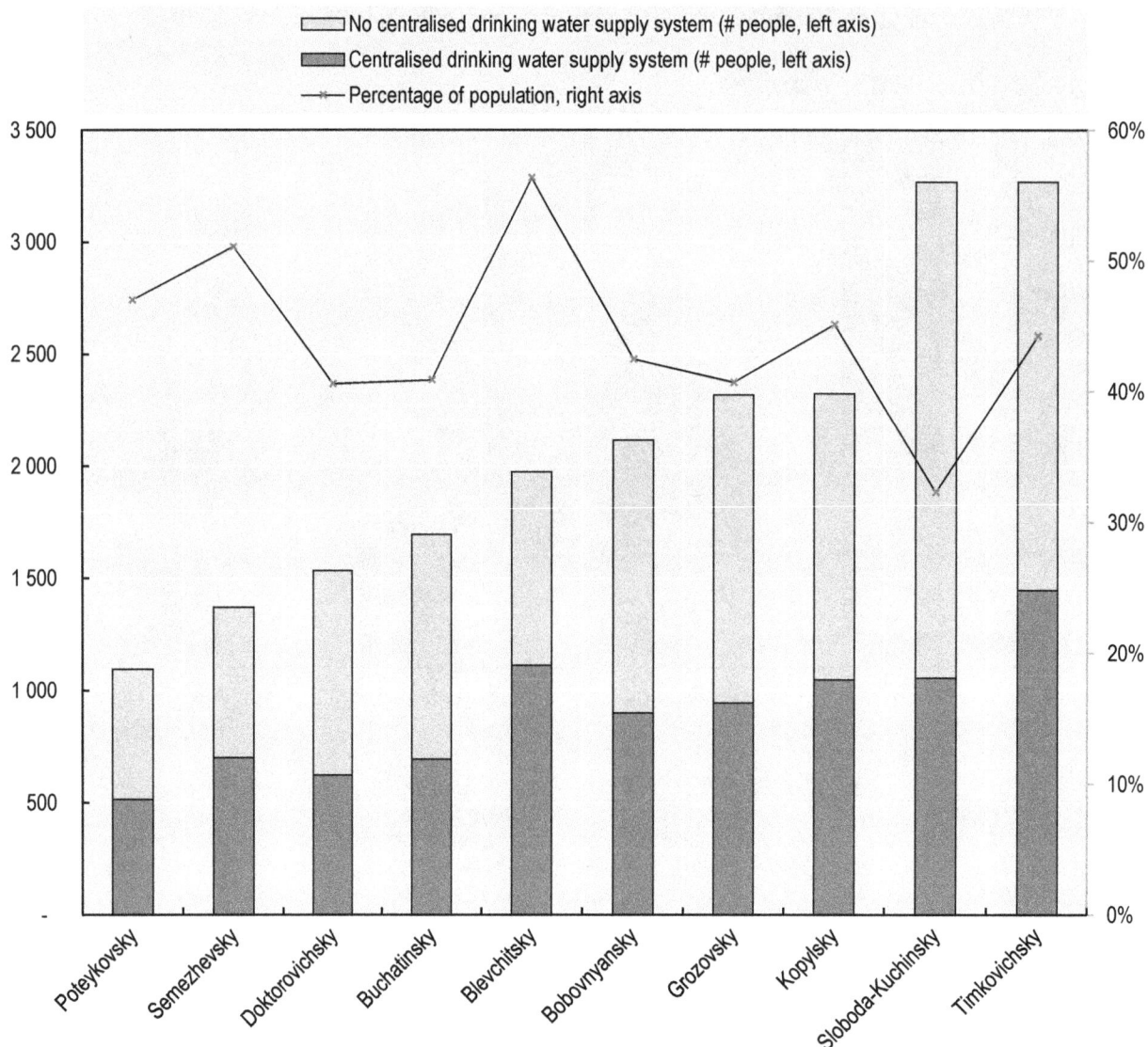

Source: CRICUWR (2019[20]), «Разработка рекомендаций по развитию систем хозяйственно-питьевого водоснабжения в Копыльском районе Минской области Беларуси» [Elaboration of Recommendations on the Development of Domestic Drinking Water Supply Systems in the Kopyl Rayon of the Minsk Oblast of Belarus], prepared by a team of experts led by P. Zakharko from the Central Research Institute for Complex Use of Water Resources, Ministry of Natural Resources and Environmental Protection of the Republic of Belarus.

Lack of centralised water supply systems in Kopyl *rayon*'s rural areas leads to unmonitored water abstractions by individuals from decentralised water supply systems (e.g. shaft wells, pipe wells). Only a small proportion of such wells are checked regularly by sanitary service. Since they lack clear ownership contracts, they are not regularly maintained and hygiene rules for potable water supply sources are often neglected (CRICUWR, 2019[20]).

Due to Kopyl *rayon*'s low population density, to extend centralised drinking water supply systems to many of its rural settlements. There, continued reliance on decentralised systems is inevitable. Half of the 208 settlements in the *rayon* have populations of 30 people or fewer, while 58 have populations of no more than 10. These smaller settlements will continue to rely on decentralised water supply systems. However, more oversight of water quality will be required to reduce health risks. For example, the water supply company should clean and maintain wells, and relevant state health authorities assure water quality control, at least once a year (CRICUWR, 2019[20]). The draft Water Strategy to 2030 includes these recommendations and mechanisms to monitor their implementation.

Water extracted from shallow wells is more likely to be contaminated by agricultural pollutants, particularly nitrates, which could make water unfit for human consumption. This led to a recommendation that boreholes reach depths of 70-90 m (CRICUWR, 2019[20]).

Kopyl's centralised water supply infrastructure does not serve the entire population of the district. However, it has significant overcapacity in terms of its water supply stations and borehole pumps. Its water supply stations have installed capacity of 10 000 m^3/day, but supply less than one-tenth of this amount on average (800 m^3/day). Its boreholes can also supply much higher volumes of water than required by the populations connected to them. For instance, the village of Lesnoye has a pump that can produce 18 480 m^3/month. However, its actual usage rate in 2017 was 12 times lower – just 1 500 m^3/month at most. Such overcapacity requires intermittent operation of the pumps, which increases operational costs and, unless proper maintenance is provided, contributes to their deterioration (Bordeniuc, 2018[21]).

The groundwater of Kopyl *rayon*, as is typical in Belarus, has high concentrations of iron. Outside of Kopyl city, the *rayon* only has two iron removal stations. Both belong to Kopyl Housing and Public Utilities and function far below their maximum capacity (2 000 m^3/day compared to 10 000 m^3/day) (Bordeniuc, 2018[21]). Given the high concentrations of iron in the groundwater withdrawn from all of Kopyl *rayon*'s boreholes (Figure 2.15), it is not using sufficient infrastructure to supply its population with quality drinking water.

Figure 2.15. Water quality from boreholes in Kopyl *rayon*: Iron and turbidity in mg/L

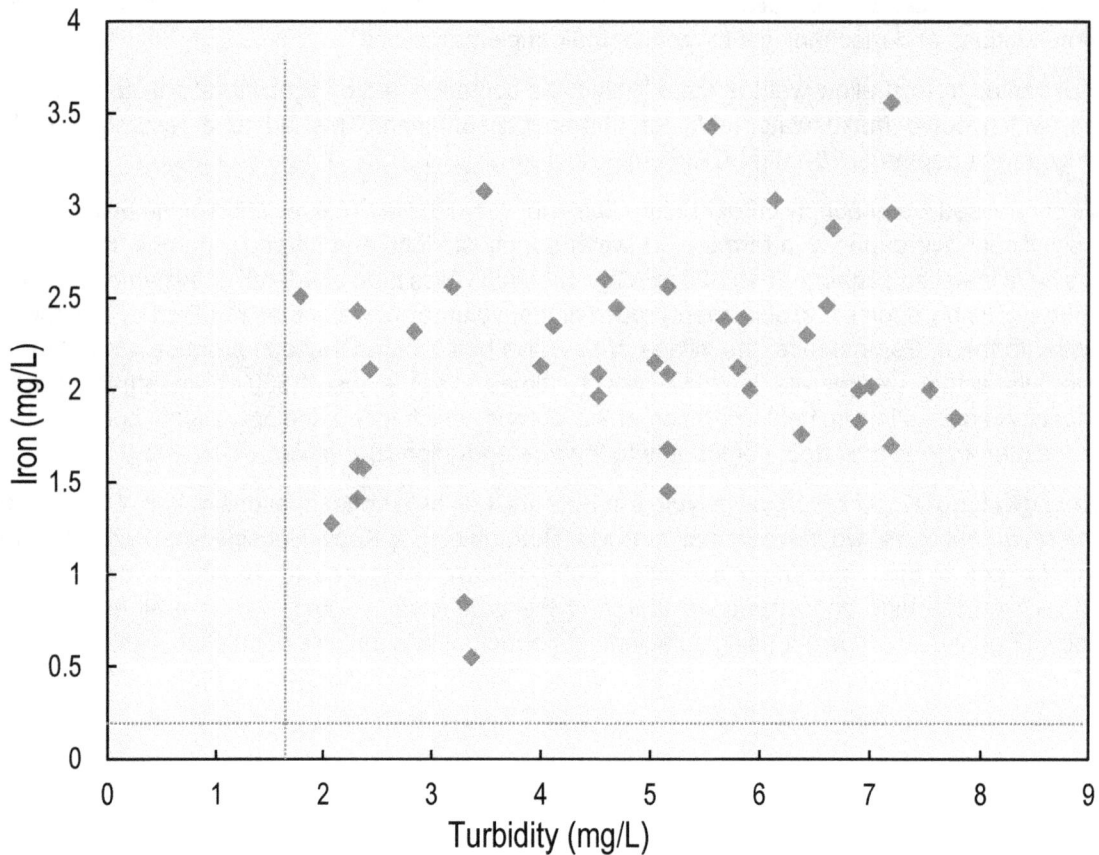

Source: Bordeniuc (2018[21]), Экспресс-обзор состояния и перспектив развития водных ресурсов и развития водохозяйственных систем в Копыльском районе Минской области Республики Беларусь [Express Survey of the Status of and Outlook for the Use of Water Resources and Development of Water Systems in the Kopyl *Rayon* of the Minsk *Oblast* of the Republic of Belarus], unpublished report prepared for the OECD under EUWI+.

2.3. Water management issues: Policy instruments and legal, regulatory and institutional frameworks

Belarus has adopted a series of policy documents that articulate its priorities for water resource management and water security.

It adopted the **Water Strategy of the Republic of Belarus to 2020** (hereafter "Water Strategy 2020)" in 2011. This was the predecessor of the draft **Strategy of Water Resource Management in the Context of Climate Change for the Period until 2030** (hereafter "Water Strategy 2030"). It is the country's main sectoral strategic document for water conservation and use, focusing primarily on the following:

- development of a pricing system for water resources
- progressive adoption of energy- and resource-saving technological processes
- creation of an integrated system of permits for nature users
- adoption of best available techniques to avoid and monitor pollution
- analysis and account of the impact of natural hydrometeorological occurrences and climate change on water resources

- introduction of technologies to improve the quality of wastewater flows (Minprirody, 2011[9]).

The **National Sustainable Development Strategy of the Republic of Belarus to 2030**, as its name implies, has a broader aim of supporting sustainable development. One priority relevant to water resource management is the improvement of legislation and regulatory legal acts (sub-law regulations) for the protection of nature, as well as for the ownership, use and management of natural resources. Other key broader development planning documents include the **Socio-economic Development Programme of the Republic of Belarus for 2016-2020** and its forthcoming update **Socio-economic Development Programme of the Republic of Belarus for 2021-2025.**

The draft **Water Strategy 2030** builds on Water Strategy 2020. It was developed in accordance with the Water Code, the National Security Concept and the National Sustainable Development Strategy to 2030. In compliance with the UNECE Protocol on SEA, and the EU SEA and Environmental Impact Assessment s, the draft Water Strategy 2030 underwent a complete SEA process supported by EUWI+. The draft strategy sets the achievement of long-term water security for current and future generations as its main strategic goal. In terms of international commitments, its objectives are linked directly to the relevant Sustainable Development Goals (Minprirody, 2018[1]).

Environment-focused documents include the Environmental Protection Strategy of the Republic of Belarus until 2025, the Strategy for the Protection and Sustainable Use of Biological Diversity for 2011-2020 and the Strategy for the Development of Scientific, Technical and Innovative Activities in the field of Environmental and the Rational Use of Natural Resources for 2014-2015 and until 2025 (Deraviaha and Dubianok, 2020[2]).

Nine national ministries participate to varying degrees in the governance of water resource protection, use and management in Belarus. This work is in addition to provincial (*oblast*-level) and local bodies (i.e. territorial bodies of the Ministry of Natural Resources and Environmental Protection, *oblast*- and *rayon*-level administrations). Although ministries' roles are clearly defined (Table 2.1), there is currently insufficient coordination between state bodies to ensure effective policy development and implementation on water protection and use. Both horizontal co-ordination (i.e. between national-level state bodies) and vertical co-ordination (i.e. between national and local structures) could be improved. The goals of different ministries in water use often conflict with one another and need to be aligned with an overarching objective (Deraviaha and Dubianok, 2020[2]).

Table 2.1. Responsibilities of ministries in Belarus related to water resource management

Ministry	Responsibilities
Ministry of Natural Resources and Environmental Protection	• carry out unified government policy on environmental protection and the rational use of natural resources • co-ordinate actions of other national state bodies in these areas
Ministry of Health	• regulate and monitor the quality of drinking water, as well as water in leisure areas
Ministry of Energy	• create and operate hydroelectric stations
Ministry of Agriculture and Food	• regulate the fish industry (fish farming and fishing) and irrigation
Ministry of Transport and Communications	• regulate the use of waterways for ships
Ministry of Housing and Communal Services	• organise centralised water supply and sanitation in settlements
Ministry of Emergency Situations	• prevent or resolve natural and anthropogenic emergency situations
Ministry of Architecture and Construction	• establish norms and requirements for the planning and construction of assets, including water infrastructure assets and buildings
Ministry of Economy	• analyse and forecast socio-economic development, planning and forecasts of sectoral and regional development.

Source: Adapted from Dereviaha, I. & S. Dubianok (2020[2]), «Экономические инструменты управления водными ресурсами и объектами и водохозяйственными системами в Республике Беларусь: тематические материалы проекта «Водная инициатива ЕС плюс для Восточного партнерства»» [Economic Instruments for the Management of Water Resources, Bodies of Water and Water Systems in the Republic of Belarus: Thematic Materials under the EU Water Initiative Plus for the Eastern Partnership], Belarusian State Technological University.

In principle, basin-level management through river basin administrations, councils and implementation of river basin management plans can improve co-ordination between government bodies to manage the use and protection of the whole basin ecosystem both ecologically and economically. On this count, Belarus has made considerable progress, especially institutionally and scientifically. Specifically, it has acted to collect qualitative and quantitative indicators; monitor and control water quality; and evaluate the condition of surface water resources. However, the role of river basin management councils needs to be expanded in the development and implementation of river basin management plans (RBMPs) (Deraviaha and Dubianok, 2020[2]). See 3.2.1.2 for more information on sound basin management.

2.3.1. Improving the use of economic instruments for water management

The introduction of "polluter pays" and "user pays" principles are prerequisites for effective river basin management. By shifting the burden onto polluters and end-users, pricing mechanisms would incentivise more efficient water use and reduced pollution.

"User pays" principle

Tariff policy is an important lever for policy makers to manage water use, but cross-subsidies in tariffs for water supply and sanitation persist, distorting price signals and economic stimuli. Policy makers should seek to gradually phase out these cross-subsidies. As real income levels rise, they should replace tariffs with targeted subsidies for particular categories of vulnerable households. These tariff adjustments go hand in hand with similar reforms in the power sector.

"Polluter pays" principle

Belarus levies an environmental tax on discharges of wastewater into the environment: into recipient surface and subsoil water bodies, both wastewater that meets non-contamination standards and wastewater purified by applying various treatment methods. The tax is based exclusively on the volume of discharged wastewater (with tax rate set in Belarusian roubles per m^3) rather than its content. In other words, the tax due does not depend on the mass of specific pollutants discharged. According to the Tax

Code of Belarus, the tax rates are differentiated. They depend on whether the wastewater (treated or meeting non-contamination standards) is discharged into a surface water body, watercourse or lake (further differentiated by river basin) or into subsoil after treatment applying nature-based biological treatment methods (at disposal/filtration fields etc.). Discharges of storm and melted waters are tax-free.

Since independence, Belarus has deviated from the Soviet pollution charge system. Under that system, polluters paid for the volume of discharged wastewaters, as well as for their composition in terms of concentrations and mass of specific pollutants. The system taxed specific water pollutants, with the rate depending on the toxicity or hazard class of the pollutant.

The present taxation of water pollution in Belarus is not optimal. First, it does not provide any economic incentives for reducing overall load of pollutants discharged into the environment. Second, it does not provide for shifting from more hazardous or toxic pollutants to less hazardous or toxic alternatives. Finally, it does not provide for applying more environmentally friendly wastewater treatment methods. A body of work was commissioned in Belarus in 2020 under the EUWI+ project to identify and assess alternative approaches to taxation of wastewater discharges.

2.3.2. Improving data management to support decision making

Belarus's water governance system does not yet feature a robust, real-time information management system. In addition to presenting ecological and water-related data, such a system would provide policy makers with the full range of information necessary to make effective decisions on water resource management. Ideally, it would present regularly updated information. To that end, it would rely on a network of institutions producing and sharing relevant data among themselves through automatic processes. It would also benefit from a platform allowing the integration and compilation of data into user-friendly information for decision makers on water resources management. Such a platform would take the form of visualisation tools and models of the country's river basins predicting their ecological status. The absence of this platform is considered a weakness in the integrated approach to data management (Deraviaha and Dubianok, 2020[2]).

Such a platform would promote stronger collaboration and knowledge exchange between different actors in the water governance sphere. The research-focused CRICUWR that works on RBMPs, operates and maintain the State Water Cadastre, for example, could work more closely with *Belhydromet*, the body subordinated to *Minprirody* and responsible for biological monitoring. See 3.2.1.1 for more details on information systems.

Such a system has several requirements:

- **Political will** with a high commitment is key to ensure good inter-institutional co-operation on data management and to establish a policy for data management and information sharing in the water sector.

- **Good governance** must rely on a combination of legislative texts (law, decree, sub-law regulation etc.) and policy; documents featuring strategies and procedures for inter-institutional co-ordination in this domain; sufficient funding of these activities and organisation of a steering committee and specific working groups to ensure information sharing.

- **A national master plan for data management in the water sector** could help develop a national water data management strategy. Such a plan could, for example, lay the foundation for a national water information system. This system would introduce procedures that reinforce the capacity of partners to manage, monitor, process and share data.

2.3.3. Improving monitoring of surface and groundwater

The monitoring of surface and groundwater systems is a key component of the EU Water Framework Directive (WFD) under Article 8:

"Member states shall ensure the establishment of programmes for the monitoring of water status in order to establish a coherent and comprehensive overview of water status within each river basin:

- for surface waters such programmes shall cover: (i) the volume and level or flow rate [...], and (ii) the ecological and chemical status and ecological potential
- for ground waters such programmes shall cover monitoring of the chemical and quantitative status."

Although Belarus has no legal obligation to comply with the WFD, the country has adopted a policy to approximate EU norms in water management. WFD Article 8 stipulates that monitoring occur "within each river basin". Consequently, good water monitoring systems require accurate delineation of water resources by river basin. Section 2.3.3.1 demonstrates the process using the Pripyat river basin as a case study, while Sections 2.3.3.2 and 2.3.3.3 discuss its monitoring system.

The Pripyat river basin was selected for a pilot project under the EUWI+ to develop an RBMP in line with WFD principles (see Box 2.1 below for information on the state of RBMPs in Belarus). The Pripyat is one of five main international river basins in Belarus that require an RBMP in line with the country's Water Code. Development of the Pripyat RBMP began in 2018. Since then, it has been delineating surface and groundwater bodies, analysing pressures and impacts, establishing environmental objectives and developing specific corrective measures. It has incorporated all surface water survey results.

Box 2.1. The status of basin planning in Belarus

During the EUWI+ inception phase in 2016, management of river basins in Belarus was still in its infancy. The country had only recently developed the first draft Dnieper river basin management plan (RBMP) for the part of the upper Dnieper basin district located on the territory of Belarus. The project, supported with assistance from the EU-funded Environmental Protection of International River Basins (EPIRB) project, was not yet implemented. The first (Dnieper) Basin Council was established in 2016. The pilot Dnieper RBMP, originally developed under the EPIRB project, was adopted the same year by the Ministry of Natural Resources and Environmental Protection.

The EUWI+ inception phase determined the Dnieper RBMP should be aligned with Water Framework Directive (WFD) principles, including economic analysis and studies of adaptation to climate change. Similarly, given the Pripyat is a tributary of the Dnieper, it decided the Pripyat RBMP should also be aligned with WFD principles. Finally, it was agreed the present Dnieper and Pripyat RBMPs will be the basis to develop in the future the umbrella river basin management plan for the whole Dnieper basin.

Source: EUWI+ (2017[22]), "European Union Water Initiative Plus for Eastern Partnership Countries: Final Inception Report," https://euwipluseast.eu/en/component/content/article/445-all-activities/activites-global-project-2/all-reports-global-project/310-final-inception-report-november-2017?Itemid=397

2.3.3.1. Delineation of water bodies: A case study of the Pripyat river basin

As a first step towards an effective monitoring system is delineating the boundaries of the river basin in question. The delineation typically follows the basin's surface hydrology boundary, but it should also consider groundwater aquifers (as it does for the Pripyat river basin). The size and complexity of river basins make them unwieldy to manage as a single unit. Basins are thus subdivided into sub-basin management areas, which tend to follow major hydrological boundaries. They group together water bodies that share common features, such as water-use patterns, ecosystems, biophysical conditions and socio-economic qualities (Pegram et al., 2013[23]).

Delineation of surface water bodies

The hydrographic network in the Pripyat river basin encompasses 50 900 km². It is part of the Black Sea basin, covering 25% of the country's land area. As a pilot area of the EUWI+ project, the network consists of 509 watercourses (rivers, streams, canals). It has a catchment area of more than 30 km² and 79 water reservoirs (lakes, reservoirs, ponds) with a surface area of more than 500 m². During the EUWI+ project, the hydrographic network of the Pripyat river basin was delineated into 715 surface water bodies: 636 rivers and 79 lakes (Figure 2.16).

Figure 2.16. Digitised hydrological network of the Pripyat river basin in Belarus

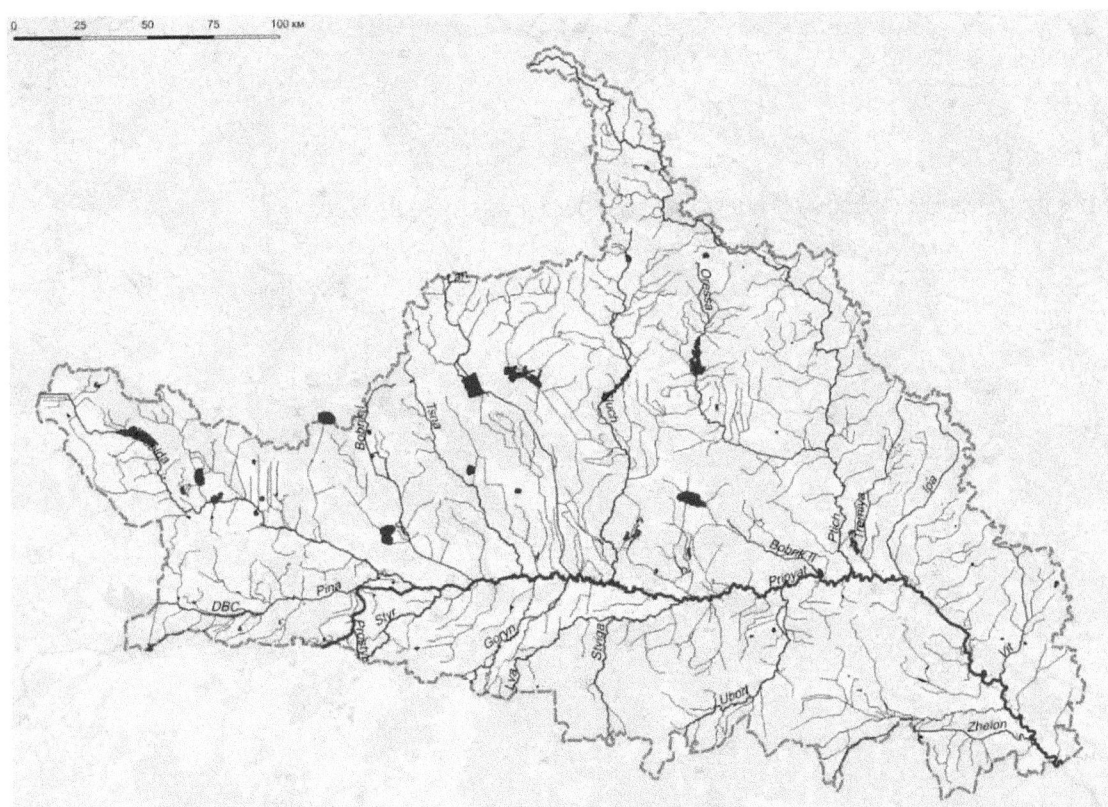

Source: EUWI+ (2020[24]), План управления бассейном реки Припять (проект) [Pripyat River Basin Management Plan (draft)], Central Research Institute for Complex Use of Water Resources (CRICUWR), Umweltbundesamt and International Office for Water, http://www.cricuwr.by/plan_pr/

In the first stage of delineation, a preliminary review of the basin attributed many surface water bodies as candidates for the "artificial water bodies" or "heavily modified water bodies" categories. This was due to their significant, permanent and irreversible hydrological or morphological modifications. For example, the basin had 735 operating drainage systems for agricultural land reclamation. The RBMP's "pressures and impacts analysis" stage assigned specific surface water bodies to the "artificial" or "highly modified" categories or as "river surface water bodies at risk" and "lake surface water bodies at risk".

The second stage of delineation was in line with the WFD's System A for characterising surface water body types[2].

The third delineation stage considered available monitoring data and information of significant human pressures. These can deteriorate the water body status (i.e. ecological and chemical status, hydrobiological and hydrochemical parameters). This led to the following results within the hydrographic network of the Pripyat river basin:

- In all, 715 surface water bodies (636 water courses and 79 water reservoirs, including lakes) were delineated, uniquely coded and documented as separate line and polygon Geographic Information System (GIS) shapefiles.

- These bodies were further categorised into 9 types of river surface water bodies and 13 types of lake surface water bodies.

- The vast majority (85.5% of river surface water bodies and 76% of lake surface water bodies) are candidates for "artificial water bodies" and "highly modified water bodies" categories due to their hydromorphological modifications (Figure 2.17).

- Only 14.5% of river surface water bodies and 24% of lake surface water bodies are close to natural conditions.

Figure 2.17. Surface water bodies in the Pripyat river basin by category

Candidates for artificial water bodies in orange; highly modified water bodies in purple

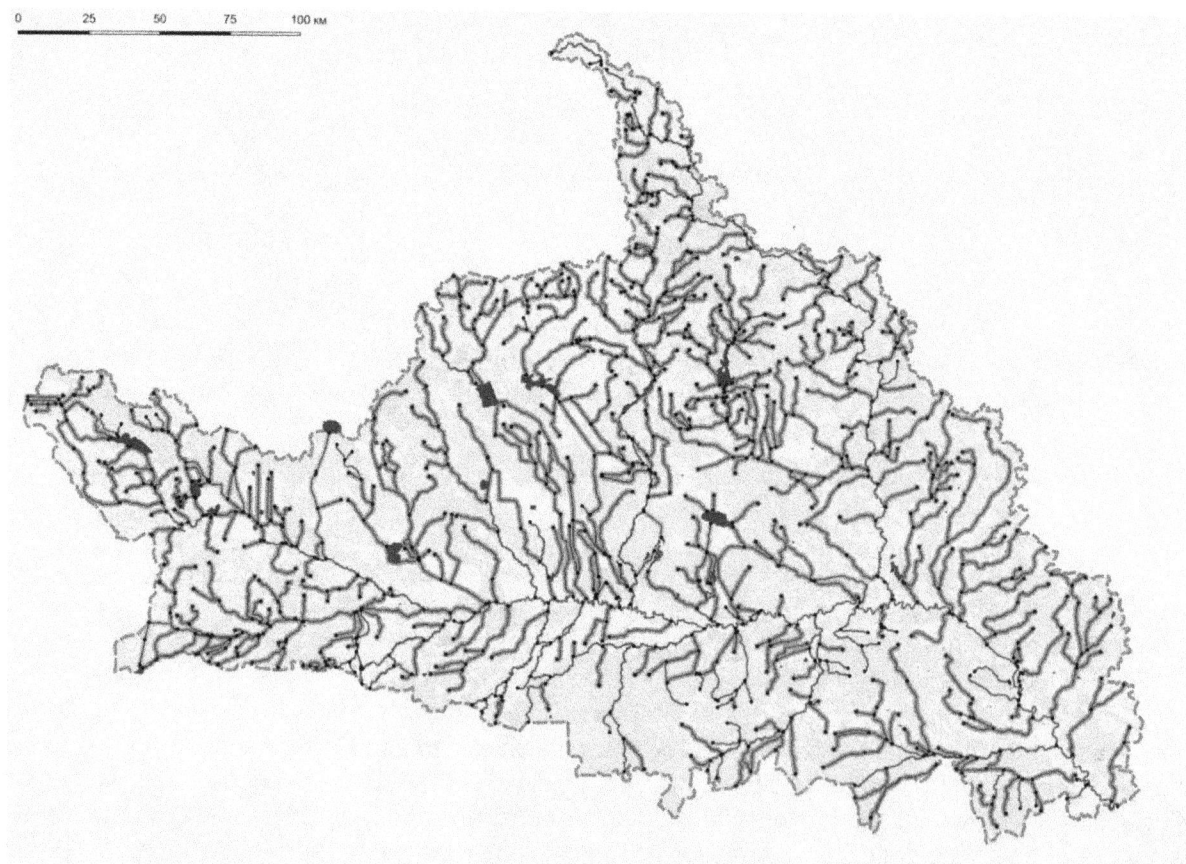

Source: EUWI+ (2020[24]), План управления бассейном реки Припять (проект) [Pripyat River Basin Management Plan (draft)], Central Research Institute for Complex Use of Water Resources (CRICUWR), Umweltbundesamt and International Office for Water, http://www.cricuwr.by/plan_pr/

Delineation of groundwater bodies

In 2018, with the help of EUWI+, the groundwater aquifers in the Pripyat river basin district were divided into 11 groups of groundwater bodies, which are the management units according to the principles of the WFD. The delineation was based on geological structure, hydrogeological conditions, lithology, flow directions or river catchments and human pressures on the aquifers. The groundwater body types are shallow (five), deep (five) and local (one) (Table 2.2).

Table 2.2. Groundwater bodies of the Pripyat river basin

Groundwater body types	Number	Number of sub-bodies	Total area, km²
Shallow (quaternary)	5	15	65 436.53
Deep	5	9	99 149.82
Local	1	1	1 407.37
Total	11	25	165 993.72
Groundwater bodies associated with ecosystems	2	7	36 096.33
Transboundary groundwater bodies	5	11	132 702.12
Groundwater bodies with quantitative monitoring	10	19	147 472.33
Groundwater bodies with quality monitoring	10	19	147 472.33

Source: EUWI+ (2020[24]), План управления бассейном реки Припять (проект) [Pripyat River Basin Management Plan (draft)], Central Research Institute for Complex Use of Water Resources (CRICUWR), Umweltbundesamt and International Office for Water, http://www.cricuwr.by/plan_pr/

This delineation is the foundation for the monitoring network and risk management, setting the stage for the Pripyat RBMP's programme of measures.

The size of the delineated groundwater bodies varies between 2 500 and 45 500 km², including overlapping areas. The shallow groundwater bodies are of a lowland nature and much influenced by, and important for, associated aquatic ecosystems and the numerous and widespread dependent terrestrial ecosystems (wetlands). Since, by definition, the groundwater levels of these shallow bodies are not deep, they lack protection against human activities on the surface, particularly agriculture. The deep groundwater bodies are well protected and overlaid by shallow groundwater bodies and confining layers. As these groundwater bodies are unpolluted and of good water quality, they are the preferred main sources for potable water supply.

Five groundwater bodies are linked with counterparts in the Dnieper (Dnipro) river basin downstream, located in Ukraine. In 2019, Belarus and Ukraine co-ordinated and harmonised the delineation of their transboundary groundwater bodies with the support of EUWI+.

2.3.3.2. Surface water monitoring

The surface water monitoring system in the Pripyat river basin only partially meets the WFD criteria. The system consists of operational, surveillance and investigative monitoring sites, but site selection could be improved using criteria provided by EUWI+.

Surface water surveys in the Pripyat river basin

The EUWI+ project supported three rounds of surface water surveys on two topics. The first topic was macroinvertebrates supplemented by assessed chemical parameters and hydromorphological site protocols. In addition, Belarus carried out a hydromorphological assessment for the first time in this same way. The first surface water field survey was conducted in October 2018 in the Pripyat river basin. It analysed 23 surface water samples from 23 monitoring sites in the chemical laboratory of the Republican Centre for Analytical Control in the Area of Environmental Protection (RACA). Biologists from CRICUWR also analysed the samples. The protocols of the ecological status of the investigated water ecosystems ranged from potential reference conditions to water bodies at risk of failing WFD environmental objectives. In June 2019, a second round was carried out at 38 sampling sites.

The survey documentation includes photographs, water and sediment samples, chemical and biological analyses, a hydromorphological description of the sampling sites and reporting of the results.

In 2019, a third hydromorphological survey was conducted at 39 sites in the Pripyat river basin to support development of the Pripyat RBMP. Prior to the field work a large amount of supporting information and documentation was prepared. This includes topographic maps and historical maps, aerial photographs and maps of web services, actual land-use information, geological maps and available long-term hydrological data.

After comparing hydrological parameters of the 39 sites such as mean flow, low flow, water-level range and frequent flow fluctuation with natural conditions, it assigned a hydrological score. It also compared morphological parameters of the 39 sites (e.g. channel sites, in-stream features, bank and riparian features, and floodplain features) with natural conditions and assigned them a morphological score. The combination of the hydrological and the morphological scores informs the hydromorphological assessment.

Conclusions of surface water surveys

The studied water bodies in the Pripyat basin have high variability. The second-year survey made progress regarding site selection, namely the inclusion of potential reference sites (in terms of pollution). Additionally, it introduced AQEM[3] codes. Since some taxonomic uncertainties persist, newer identification keys will be provided. Biological monitoring can be improved by an ecological status classification system based on the pressure-impact relationship.

The chemical laboratories of RACA were not accredited for tests, including for analysing total dissolved phosphorus, acid neutralising capacity and laboratory practices.

The surveys selected qualitative samples of macroinvertebrates based on recommendations of several techniques developed in EU member countries. The latter considered regional characteristics of watercourses (e.g. lowland rivers with low velocity). They carried out representative sampling at all habitats such as sandy sediment with varying proportion of silt, stands of submerged and semi-submerged macrophytes and stony-sandy sediment. The analyses of macroinvertebrates from rivers of the Pripyat basin (June 2019) identified 211 species and aquatic organisms belonging to 76 different families and 7 major groups.

A comparison of similar sites between 2018 and 2019 indicates that results are highly reproducible and that controlled sections of watercourses are stable. The number of bottom macroinvertebrates varied from 16-45 species and forms in 2018, while 15-56 species and forms were found in 2019. The larvae of emerging insects (mainly *Chironomidae*) determined the basis of variability; this is associated with the seasonal dynamics of larval development and mass flight of imagos. Small and medium watercourses had the highest variability of indicators since their ecosystems are more sensitive to natural or anthropogenic stress.

The hydromorphological assessment classified 39 sampling sites into the following categories: 2 (~5%) as "high", 10 (~25%) as "good", 7 (~19%) as "moderate" and 20 (~51%) as "poor".

The results are included into the "hydromorphological assessment chapter" of the draft Pripyat RBMP. They will also be considered during the development of policy measures. Finally, they will help with ecological classification of the sampling sites covered by the EUWI+ project.

The experience and practice obtained during the EUWI+ project pilot surveys and assessment in the Pripyat river basin have potential for replication. This could include sharing lessons learned across the wider river basin and in the other main river basins in Belarus and in other EaP countries.

2.3.3.3. Groundwater monitoring

In Belarus, groundwater plays a key role in drinking water supply and is essential for the numerous wetlands that depend on shallow groundwater. Regular monitoring of the quantitative and chemical state of groundwater is therefore essential. Data can inform appropriate management measures and guarantee long-term sustainability for human use, as well as associated aquatic and dependent terrestrial ecosystems.

Belarus has monitored groundwater since the 1960s. Initially, it focused mainly on the effects of the reclamation of wetlands on groundwater quantity. In the 1970s and 1980s, monitoring also considered the impact of human activities on groundwater quality.

The State Groundwater Observation Network has three goals. First, it aims to identify the status of groundwater. Second, it seeks to forecast changes that might result in negative impacts. Third, it aims to determine the impact of measures that were designed to maintain the status of the groundwater. Therefore, groundwater monitoring is observing the natural, undisturbed conditions, the disturbed groundwater regime (disturbed by groundwater abstractions) and local pollution effects.

A review of the groundwater monitoring design within the territory of the Pripyat river basin in 2018 identified several proposals for improvement. At present, groundwater quantity and chemicals are monitored within the Pripyat basin at 26 hydrogeological posts representing the natural groundwater regime (with 76 wells); at 44 water intakes representing the disturbed groundwater regime (with 111 wells); and at 35 objects of local groundwater monitoring representing point sources of pollution (314 observation wells).

The EUWI+ project has divided groundwater aquifers in the Pripyat river basin into 11 groundwater management units ("groundwater bodies"), according to WFD principles. According to this new distinction, the monitoring network covers only 8 of these 11 groundwater bodies. This network needs to be extended for some groundwater bodies. Therefore, it recommended 14 new monitoring wells in four groundwater bodies.

Groundwater quantity is monitored at almost all observation points three times a month. In all, 13 of the 76 wells are equipped with automatic level gauges. In principle, groundwater chemical monitoring is to be performed once per year for a list of parameters/indicators. However, due to lack of funding it is not conducted at all observation wells. For example, in 2016, chemical monitoring was conducted at 57 wells in natural regime and in 2018 at 10 of 76 wells.

In 2019, EUWI+ supported a special study on the shallow groundwater body (BYPRGW0001, a Holocene swamp aquifer), which is not covered by any groundwater monitoring. This groundwater is not used for drinking water. However, since swamps cover 23% of the territory of the Pripyat river basin district it has a significant influence on adjacent groundwater aquifers, associated aquatic ecosystems and groundwater-dependent terrestrial ecosystems. The study proposed integrating new monitoring sites into pre-existing sites to be easily integrated into the State Groundwater Observation Network. The study was accompanied by a groundwater survey covering 15 existing wells and a comprehensive list of substances, including 20 pesticides. The monitoring results reflect very well the influence of the swamps, but also the influence of agriculture pollution in areas that were previously drained. No pesticides were found.

EUWI+ supported a special study in 2019 on the impacts of the Petrikov dump sites of unusable pesticides on groundwater bodies in this area. Between 1974 and 1988, a significant amount of unusable pesticides was stored in the northern part of the Petrikov *rayon* (Gomel *oblast*). This study also explored the radiation impacts of the Chernobyl Nuclear Power Plant accident on the groundwater bodies in the southeast of the

Pripyat river basin. Groundwater samples from 14 monitoring sites were analysed on a comprehensive list of substances that included organochlorine pesticides, strontium-90 and caesium-137. The monitoring results of the southeast of the Pripyat basin showed no traces of these substances in the corresponding groundwater bodies. All 7 wells show pesticide concentrations around the Petrikov dump sites, but only 1 of the 20 analysed pesticide substances exceeded the permissible standard in a single well.

2.4. Transboundary co-operation on water resources

At any transboundary river basin, knowledge and data exchange, along with joint monitoring, are of utmost importance for sound and harmonised large-scale water management. A transboundary pilot survey and sub-regional workshops for knowledge exchange are first steps towards inter-calibration of ecological status classification systems.

Belarus has been a Party to the UNECE Convention on the Protection and Use of Transboundary Watercourses and International Lakes since 2003. The Convention serves as a model for agreements and arrangements in the field of transboundary river basin management. Belarus is one of about 50 countries worldwide with more than 75% of its territory covered by transnational river basins. Transnational river basins cover all of Belarus's territory as all of the country's large rivers (defined as longer than 500 km) are transboundary with the notable exception of the Berezina river (Deraviaha and Dubianok, 2020[2]). Transboundary co-operation is thus particularly important. All of its neighbouring countries are also Parties to this Convention, which provides a good basis for cross-border co-operation.

Prior to the EUWI+ programme, Belarus had intergovernmental agreements on the protection and use of transboundary waters with Russia and Ukraine. Within the framework of these agreements, working groups address various cross-border issues. In addition, there is a Technical Protocol between the Ministry of Natural Resources and Environmental Protection of Belarus and the Ministry of the Environment of Lithuania to co-operate in monitoring and exchange of information on the state of transboundary surface waters. In February 2020, the Government of the Republic of Belarus signed a co-operation agreement with the Government of Poland on the protection and rational use of transboundary waters. At the time of drafting this report, the Agreement was submitted for ratification.

Notes

[1] The population of Belarus in 2018 was 4.96% smaller than in 2000 (and 6.92% smaller than in 1990). Similar but more pronounced population changes occurred in Lithuania (24.6% smaller than in 1990; 20.29% smaller than in 2000), Latvia (27.4% smaller than in 1990; 18.6% smaller than in 2000), Bulgaria (19.5% smaller than in 1990, 14.1% smaller than in 2000), Romania (16.1% smaller than in 1990; 13.2% smaller than in 2000), Ukraine (14.0% smaller than in 1990; 9.3% smaller than in 2000) and Serbia (8.0% smaller than 1990; 7.2% smaller than 2000). Belarus's experience is most similar to that of Hungary (5.8% smaller than 1990; 4.3% smaller than 2000) and Poland (0.3% smaller than 1990; 0.7% smaller than 2000) (World Bank, 2020[11]).

[2] System A is one of the two methods for classifying surface water body types defined by the EU's Water Framework Directive (WFD). It uses features such as ecoregion, altitude, size, geology and depth (for lakes). For more details, see Annex II of the WFD.

[3] AQEM refers to the Development and Testing of an Integrated Assessment System for the Ecological Quality of Streams and Rivers throughout Europe using Benthic Macroinvertebrates project. For more information, see http://aqem.de/

References

Belstat (2019), *С.3. Водопотребление [C.3. Water Consumption]*, (database), https://www.belstat.gov.by/ofitsialnaya-statistika/makroekonomika-i-okruzhayushchaya-sreda/okruzhayuschaya-sreda/sovmestnaya-sistema-ekologicheskoi-informatsii2/c-vodnye-resursy/c-3-vodopotreblenie/   [10]

Belstat (2019), *Структура валового регионального продукта по видам экономической деятельности в 2018 году [Structure of the Gross Regional Product by Economic Activity in 2018]*, (database), https://www.belstat.gov.by/ofitsialnaya-statistika/realny-sector-ekonomiki/natsionalnye-scheta/graficheskiy-material-grafiki-diagrammy/struktura-valovogo-regionalnogo-produkta-po-vidam-ekonomicheskoy-deyatelnosti-v-2017-godu/ (accessed on 31 March 2020).   [19]

Belstat (2019), *Численность населения по областям и г. Минску [Population by Region and the City of Minsk]*, (database), https://www.belstat.gov.by/ofitsialnaya-statistika/solialnaya-sfera/naselenie-i-migratsiya/naselenie-godovye-dannye/   [18]

Belstat (2019), *Численность населения по осбластям и г. Минску [Population by Region and the City of Minsk]*, (database), https://www.belstat.gov.by/ofitsialnaya-statistika/solialnaya-sfera/naselenie-i-migratsiya/naselenie-godovye-dannye/ (accessed on 30 March 2020).   [8]

Bordeniuc, V. (2018), *Экспресс-обзор состояния и перспектив развития водных ресурсов и развития водохозяйственных систем в Копыльском районе Минской области Республики Беларусь [Express Survey of the Status of and Outlook for the Use of Water Resources and Development of Water Systems in the Kopyl District of the Minsk Region of the Republic of Belarus]*, unpublished report prepared for the OECD under EUWI+.   [21]

CRICUWR (2019), *Государственный водный кадастр: Водные ресурсы, их использование и качество вод (за 2018 год) [State Water Cadastre: Water Resources, Their Use and Water Quality (in 2018)]*, Central Research Institute for Complex Use of Water Resources, Ministry of Natural Resources and Environmental Protection of the Republic of Belarus, Minsk.   [7]

CRICUWR (2019), *Разработка рекомендаций по развитию систем хозяйственно-питьевого водоснабжения в Копыльском районе Минской области Беларуси [Elaboration of Recommendations on the Development of Domestic Drinking Water Supply]*, Central Research Institute for Complex Use of Water Resources, Ministry of Natural Resources and Environmental Protection of the Republic of Belarus, Minsk.   [20]

Deraviaha, I. and S. Dubianok (2020), *Экономические инструменты управления водными ресурсами и объектами и водохозяйственными системами в Республике Беларусь: тематические материалы проекта «Водная инициатива ЕС плюс для Восточного партнерства» [Economic instruments for the Management of Water Resources, Bodies of Water and Water Systems in the Republic of Belarus: Thematic Materials under the EU Water Initiative Plus for the Eastern Partnership]*, Belarusian State Technological University, Minsk.   [2]

European Environment Agency (2018), "C2 – Freshwater Abstraction in Georgia", *ENI SEIS II East*, (database), https://eni-seis.eionet.europa.eu/east/indicators/c2-2013-freshwater-abstraction-in-georgia   [14]

Eurostat (2020), *Fresh Water Abstraction by Source - million m³*, (database), [17]
https://ec.europa.eu/eurostat/databrowser/view/ten00002/default/table?lang=en

EUWI+ (2020), *План управления бассейном реки Припять (проект) [Pripyat River Basin* [24]
Management Plan (draft)], Central Research Institute for Complex Use of Water Resources
(CRICUWR), Umweltbundesamt and International Office for Water,
http://www.cricuwr.by/plan_pr/ (accessed on 29 July 2020).

EUWI+ (2017), *European Union Water Initiative Plus for Eastern Partnership Countries: Final* [22]
Inception Report, UNECE, OECD, Umweltbundesamt and International Office for Water,
https://euwipluseast.eu/en/component/content/article/445-all-activities/activites-global-project-
2/all-reports-global-project/310-final-inception-report-november-2017?Itemid=397.

FAO (n.d.), "Sustainable Development Goals: Indicator 6.4.2 - Level of Water Stress: Freshwater [5]
Withdrawal as a Proportion of Available Freshwater Resources", webpage,
http://www.fao.org/sustainable-development-goals/indicators/642/en/ (accessed on
30 March 2020).

Minprirody (2018), *Стратегия управления водными ресурсами в условиях изменения* [1]
климата на период до 2030 года (проект) [The Strategy of Water Resource Management
in the Context of Climate Change Adaptation for the Period Until 2030: Draft], Central
Research Institute for Complex Use of Water Resources, Ministry of Natural Resources and
Environmental Protection of the Republic of Belarus, Minsk.

Minprirody (2011), *Водная стратегия Республики Беларусь на период до 2020 года [Water* [9]
Strategy of the Republic of Belarus for the Period to 2020], Central Research Institute for
Complex Use of Water Resources, Ministry of Natural Resources and Environmental
Protection of the Republic of Belarus, Minsk,
http://www.minpriroda.gov.by/ru/new_url_1649710582-ru/ (accessed on 30 March 2020).

Pegram, G. et al. (2013), *River Basin Planning: Principles, Procedures and Approaches for* [23]
Strategic Basin Planning, UNESCO, Paris,
https://www.gwp.org/globalassets/global/toolbox/references/river-basin-planning.pdf.

State Statistical Committee of the Republic of Azerbaijan (2020), *9.1. Su ehtiyatlarının* [13]
mühafizəsini və onlardan istifadə edilməsini səciyyələndirən əsas göstəricilər [9.1. Key
Indicators Characterising the Protection and Use of Water Resources], (database),
https://www.stat.gov.az/source/environment/az/009_1.xls

Statistica Moldovei (2019), "The Main Indicators of Water Use, 2001-2018", *Water Use*, [15]
(database),
http://statbank.statistica.md/PxWeb/pxweb/en/10%20Mediul%20inconjurator/10%20Mediul%
20inconjurator__MED020/MED020100.px/

Statistical Committee of the Republic of Armenia (2020), "Water Abstraction, mln. m3 / 2020", [12]
Time Series, (database), https://www.armstat.am/en/?nid=12&id=14004&submit=Search

Ukrstat (2018), *Main Indicators on the Water Resources Use and Protection*, (database), [16]
https://ukrstat.org/en/operativ/operativ2006/ns_rik/ns_e/opvvr_rik_e2005.htm

UNECE (2016), *Belarus: Environmental Performance Reviews, Third Review*, United Nations Economic Commission for Europe, New York and Geneva, https://www.unece.org/fileadmin/DAM/env/epr/epr_studies/ECE.CEP.178_Eng.pdf (accessed on 30 March 2020). [3]

UNITER (2016), *Экономика Республики Беларусь: Анализ структуры и перспективы инвестирования в отдельные отрасли [Economy of the Republic of Belarus: Analysis of the Structure and Investment Prospects in Particular Sectors]*, UNITER Investment Company, Minsk, https://www.uniter.by/upload/iblock/c8d/c8d38c0d30e65139d6aa1dbe6fd2e636.pdf. [6]

Volchek, A. et al. (2017), *Водные ресурсы Беларуси и их прогноз с учетом изменения климата [Water Resources of Belarus and Their Forecast Accounting for Climate Change]*, Alternativa, Brest. [4]

World Bank (2020), *World Development Indicators*, (database), https://data.worldbank.org/ (accessed on 26 October 2018). [11]

3 Policy responses

This chapter lays out the policy responses to the challenges identified in Chapter 2 within the context of Belarus's new draft *Strategy of Water Resource Management in the Context of Climate Change for the Period until 2030*. It describes the Strategy's development and its objectives linked to the water-related Sustainable Development Goals (SDGs). The chapter also presents instruments to support the Strategy's implementation, notably data collection and management systems, river basin management plans and the UNECE-WHO/Europe Protocol on Water and Health. The chapter zooms in on different sectoral, regional and basin-level challenges, focusing on rural water supply and sanitation, water-use efficiency standards for water-intensive enterprises, irrigation infrastructure rehabilitation and sub-basin management plans.

3.1. Support to develop Belarus's national Water Strategy to 2030

Globally, water resources are under pressure, with demand increasing six-fold over the last century. By 2025, the agriculture and energy sectors are expected to consume 60% and 80% more than current levels, respectively. As a result of climate change, water systems are becoming less predictable and reliable. Economic activity continues to compromise the quality of water resources due to pollution from industrial wastewater and runoff from agricultural facilities and human settlements. Water is inherently connected to various sectors, notably through the food-water-energy nexus; poor water infrastructure can impair the delivery of other key infrastructure services (Strelkovskii et al., 2019[1]). As demographic pressures increase and the effects of climate change become more apparent, governments need a robust, comprehensive water strategy to confront these mounting, interconnected challenges and ensure water security for all.

As part of the European Union Water Initiative Plus for the Eastern Partnership (EUWI+) project, two capacity building workshops were organised for the Republic of Belarus (hereafter "Belarus") on strategic and mid-term planning for water management. The first took place in October 2017 as a side event at the International Water Forum in Minsk, while the second occurred in April 2018. To complement these activities, the International Institute for Applied Systems Analysis in co-operation with the OECD held a training workshop in 2018. Supported by the government of Norway, the workshop explored innovative methods and tools based on systems analysis. Through a participatory approach, attendees learned to develop a "no regret" national water strategy in the context of high risks, uncertainty and conflicting interests of water users. Representatives of ministries and agencies from Belarus took part in this well-received event, along with colleagues from Georgia, Moldova and Ukraine (Strelkovskii et al., 2019[1]).

This training complemented other efforts under EUWI+ to support the development and implementation of Belarus's Strategy of Water Resource Management in the Context of Climate Change for the Period until 2030 (hereafter "Water Strategy 2030"). Belarus recognised the importance of strategic environmental assessment (SEA) for the comprehensive integration of environmental and health concerns into the legislative process. For that reason, it joined the UN Economic Commission for Europe (UNECE) Protocol on SEA. Consequently, the Ministry of Natural Resources and Environmental Protection asked UNECE to support a pilot application of SEA. The SEA process for the draft Water Strategy 2030 was implemented according to international requirements, including comprehensive public consultation, and has already resulted in significant improvements of the draft Water Strategy.

The SEA process was organised in two steps. First, a scoping SEA report was compiled and distributed for comments. This consultation took place online due to restrictions on physical meetings related to COVID-19. Second, a full SEA report was published and opened for public consultation. Comments received helped significantly improve the final SEA report, and also helped formulate valuable recommendations for the draft Water Strategy 2030.

The developers of the Water Strategy 2030 adopted several SEA recommendations from this process. These pertained to more robust sections on wetlands; the role of the protected area system in safeguarding valuable water ecosystems; expansion of protected areas and forecasts of seasonal changes in river flow; and consequences for water-dependent economic sectors and natural ecosystems.

The final SEA report concluded that the draft Water Strategy 2030 is well-linked to other strategic documents at the national level related to the use and protection of water resources. The goals in the draft Water Strategy 2030 are generally consistent with the environmental and social goals identified for each thematic component.

Overall, the Water Strategy 2030 was expected to lead to positive changes in the natural and socio-ecological environments. Potential risks are associated mostly with the planned development of water transport systems (e.g. the reconstruction of the inland waterway known as E-40), hydroelectric power, the development of centralised water supply systems and recreational activities. These risks can be mitigated or minimised through the adoption and strict application of corresponding environmental standards and mitigation measures.

The following measures were identified to reduce or prevent possible negative consequences for the environment, including some transboundary effects, during implementation of Water Strategy 2030:

- Improve water management and ensure rational use of water resources through the use of recycled water, maintaining level regime in the area of collective water withdrawals.
- Develop local monitoring systems for measuring changes in terrestrial and aquatic ecosystems.
- Develop and apply methods for classification and valuation of water-related ecosystem services.
- Consider the vulnerability of soils to droughts, especially under changing climatic conditions, when planning measures for the protection of water resources and their rational use.
- Develop a methodology for monitoring pollution of water bodies caused by application of fertilisers, plant protection products and other chemicals used for agricultural production.
- Strengthen the monitoring system with assessment of ecosystem dynamics, invasive species of plants and animals, dynamics of forest areas and monitoring of hydrophilic species populations.

To minimise negative environmental consequences of planned hydroelectric power plants, particular attention should be given to protected areas, Ramsar sites, key ornithological territories and other territories and water bodies important for biodiversity conservation.

The implementing partners of EUWI+ helped the government of Belarus ensure the new strategy was aligned with relevant national legislation and planning documents. These included the Water Code and the National Strategy for Sustainable Socio-economic Development. They also sought to align the strategy with international commitments.[1] The resulting draft strategy is a robust, comprehensive document, satisfying most of the criteria highlighted by a key study (Strelkovskii et al., 2019[1]) for national water strategies (Table 3.1).

Table 3.1. A checklist for Water Strategy 2030

Criteria for an effective, comprehensive water strategy	Water Strategy 2030
• Covers both water resources and aquatic ecosystems, and water infrastructure	Yes
• Considers best practices and international principles, guidelines and good practices	Somewhat
o EU WFD	Yes
o UNECE Water Convention on the Protection and Use of Transboundary Watercourses and International Lakes	Yes
o UNECE-WHO Regional Office for Europe Protocol on Water and Health	Yes
• Links to other key policies such as:	Yes
o National Strategy for Sustainable Development	Yes
o Sectoral strategies	Yes
• Should combine up to four time horizons:	Yes, 3
o Strategic (50-100 years)	No
o Mid-term (7-30 years)	Yes
o Short-term (3-7 years)	Yes
o Workplans for immediate actions (1-3 years)	Yes
• Should include:	Some
o Diagnosis (current state, trends, main challenges, risks, uncertainties)	Yes
o Definition of desired future (strategic objectives, targets)	Yes
o Preferred and alternative scenarios	No
o Information on the interests of stakeholders and what choices impact them	No
o Implementation plan	Yes

Source: Strekovskii et al. (2019[1]), "Navigating through Deep Waters of Uncertainty: Systems Analysis Approach to Strategic Planning of Water Resources and Water Infrastructure under High Uncertainties and Conflicting Interests", International Institute for Applied Systems Analysis and the OECD; CRICUWR (2018[2]), Стратегия управления водными ресурсами в условиях изменения климата на период до 2030 года (проект) [The Strategy of Water Resource Management in the Context of Climate Change for the Period Until 2030: Draft], Central Research Institute for Complex Use of Water Resources, Ministry of Natural Resources and Environmental Protection of the Republic of Belarus.

Water Strategy 2030's primary objectives echo the targets for the Sustainable Development Goals (SDGs), which are noted in brackets after the relevant objective below:

1. Supply 100% of Belarus's population with drinking water and water disposal services in line with safety standards (SDG 6.1 & SDG 6.2).
2. Improve the quality of Belarus's water bodies (SDG 6.3).
3. Increase the efficiency of water use (SDG 6.4).
4. Implement integrated water resources management (SDG 6.5).
5. Protect Belarus's aquatic ecosystems (SDG 6.6).
6. Exploit untapped water use potential (e.g. for water transport, HEPPs, bottled mineral water) (Minprirody, 2018[3]).

By ensuring water security, Water Strategy 2030 is a means to achieve SDG 6.

In terms of SDGs 6.1 ("By 2030, achieve universal and equitable access to safe and affordable drinking water for all") and 6.2 ("By 2030, achieve access to adequate and equitable sanitation and hygiene for all and end open defecation…"), Belarus has already made considerable progress. It has extended safe water and sanitation services to its population. The percentage of citizens benefiting from access to clean drinking water increased from 77.7% to 95.4% over 2000-18 (Figure 3.1). As discussed in Section 2.2.4, however, rural populations are significantly less likely to have a universal access to safe drinking water supply, water disposal and sanitation services as envisaged by SDG 6.1 and 6.2. Water Strategy 2030 recognises the particular challenges facing rural communities.

Figure 3.1. Access to centralised water supply and wastewater treatment has improved over the past two decades in Belarus

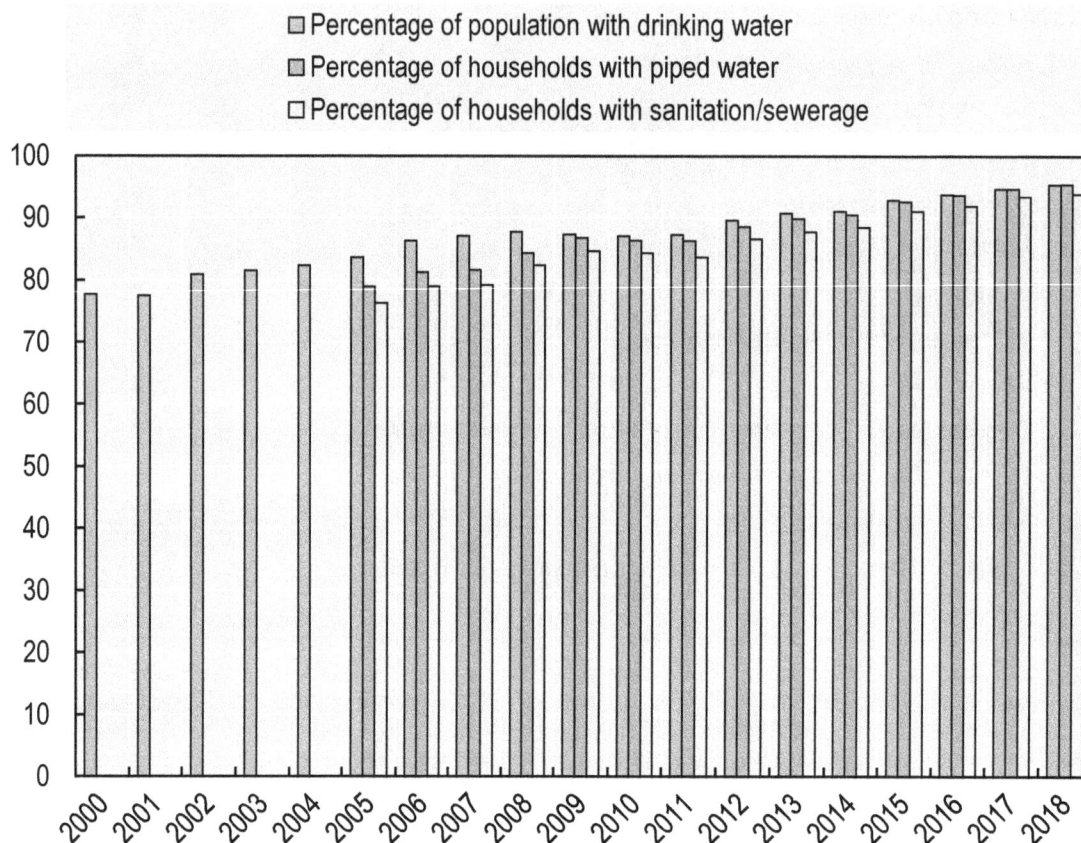

Source: Belstat (2019[4]), «*С.5. Вода, поставляемая отраслью водоснабжения, и доступ населения к этой воде*» [C.5. Water Provided by the Water Supply Industry and Access of the Population to that Water] (database), National Statistical Committee of the Republic of Belarus, www.belstat.gov.by/ofitsialnaya-statistika/makroekonomika-i-okruzhayushchaya-sreda/okruzhayuschaya-sreda/sovmestnaya-sistema-ekologicheskoi-informatsii2/c-vodnye-resursy/s-5-voda-postavlyaemaya-otraslyu-vodosnabzheniya-i-dostup-naseleniya-k-etoi-vode/; Belstat (2019[5]), «*С.6. Доступ населения к централизованному водоснабжению*» [C.6. Access of the Population to Centralised Water Supply] (database), National Statistical Committee of the Republic of Belarus, www.belstat.gov.by/ofitsialnaya-statistika/makroekonomika-i-okruzhayushchaya-sreda/okruzhayuschaya-sreda/sovmestnaya-sistema-ekologicheskoi-informatsii2/c-vodnye-resursy/s-6-dostup-naseleniya-k-tsentralizovannomu-vodosnabzheniyu/; Belstat (2019[6]), «*С.14. Население, обеспеченное очисткой сточных вод*» [C. 14. Population Connected to Wastewater Treatment] (database), National Statistical Committee of the Republic of Belarus, www.belstat.gov.by/ofitsialnaya-statistika/makroekonomika-i-okruzhayushchaya-sreda/okruzhayuschaya-sreda/sovmestnaya-sistema-ekologicheskoi-informatsii2/c-vodnye-resursy/s-14-naselenie-obespechennoe-ochistkoi-stochnyh-vod/.

For SDGs 6.3-6.5, EUWI+, together with the government of Belarus, has supported nationalisation of the indicators for specific tasks under the goals and the development and adoption of national indicator monitoring framework for measuring progress towards these targets. "Nationalisation" refers to the definitions of indicators (or nationally adopted proxy indicators) and formation of national methodologies for calculating indicators. In the case of Belarus, these indicators are those associated with SDG targets 6.3, 6.4 and 6.5: 6.3.1, 6.3.2, 6.4.1, 6.4.2, 6.5.1 and 6.5.2. These methodologies were agreed upon with the National Statistical Committee of the Republic of Belarus and other stakeholders of the bodies of state administration and organisations. They were subsequently discussed at the meeting of the Inter-departmental Expert Group on Environmental Guidelines for Achieving Sustainable Development Goals in October 2019. They were approved by the Ministry of Natural Resources and Environmental Protection of the Republic of Belarus in November 2019. As shown in Table 3.2, indicators 6.4.2 and 6.5.1 have been fully nationalised, while the remaining indicators (and particularly 6.3.2) require further development. Table 3.3 presents the status of indicator nationalisation achieved by Belarus's neighbouring countries.

Table 3.2. Progress on nationalisation of SDG 6.3-6.5

	Custodian agency/agencies	Level of nationalisation (1 = best, 3 = worst)
Target 6.3: By 2030, improve water quality by reducing pollution, eliminating dumping and minimising release of hazardous chemicals and materials, halving the proportion of untreated wastewater and substantially increasing recycling and safe reuse globally		
6.3.1 Proportion of wastewater flow safely treated	WHO, UN Habitat	2
6.3.2 Proportion of water bodies with good ambient water quality	UNEP	3
Target 6.4: By 2030, substantially increase water-use efficiency across all sectors and ensure sustainable withdrawals and supply of freshwater to address water scarcity and substantially reduce the number of people suffering from water scarcity		
6.4.1 Change in water-use efficiency over time	FAO	2
6.4.2 Level of water stress: Freshwater withdrawal as a proportion of available freshwater resources	FAO	1
Target 6.5: By 2030, implement integrated water resources management at all levels, including through transboundary co-operation as appropriate		
6.5.1 Degree of integrated water resources management implementation (from 0 to 100)	UNEP	1
6.5.2 Proportion of transboundary basin area with an operational arrangement for water co-operation	UNECE, UNESCO	2

Notes: FAO = Food and Agriculture Organization of the United Nations; UNECE = UN Economic Commission for Europe; UNEP = UN Environment Programme.

Source: CRICUWR (2018[7]), «Помощь правительству Беларуси в национализации индикаторов для мониторинга прогресса в реализации SDG 6.3 – 6.5» [Assistance to the Government of Belarus in the Nationalisation of Indicators for the Monitoring of Progress Towards Achieving SDG 6.3-6.5], prepared by a team of experts led by S. Dubianok from the Central Research Institute for Complex Use of Water Resources, Ministry of Natural Resources and Environmental Protection of the Republic of Belarus.

Table 3.3. Progress towards nationalising SDG 6.3-6.5 indicators in neighbouring countries

	Russian Federation	Ukraine	Poland	Lithuania	Latvia
6.3.1	Yes (2016)	Proxy (2015)	Yes (2010-16)	Proxy (2010-16)	Proxy (2010-16)
6.3.2	No	Proxy (2015)	Yes (2015, lakes)	Yes (2010-16)	Proxy (2010-16)
6.4.1	No	Proxy (2015)	Proxy (2010-15)	No	Proxy
6.4.2	No	Proxy (2015)	Proxy (2010-15)	Proxy (2010-15)	Proxy (2010-15)
6.5.1	No	Proxy (2015)	No	No	Proxy
6.5.2	No	No	Yes (2013-16)	No	Proxy
Periodicity of review	Annual	Every 5 years (2015, 2020, 2025, 2030)	Annual, except 6.3.2 (every 6 years)	Annual	2020, 2030

Source: CRICUWR (2018[7]), «Помощь правительству Беларуси в национализации индикаторов для мониторинга прогресса в реализации SDG 6.3 – 6.5» [Assistance to the Government of Belarus in the Nationalisation of Indicators for the Monitoring of Progress Towards Achieving SDG 6.3-6.5], prepared by a team of experts led by S. Dubianok from the Central Research Institute for Complex Use of Water Resources, Ministry of Natural Resources and Environmental Protection of the Republic of Belarus.

3.2. Support to implement the Water Strategy

3.2.1. Instruments

3.2.1.1. Sound database for informed decision making

Access to accurate, reliable datasets is a prerequisite for effective water resource management. Belarus, like many countries, always collects, manages and processes relevant datasets. However, many different institutions are involved. This makes good inter-institutional co-operation on data management essential to ensure efficient access for decision makers. An effective policy is needed to reinforce synergies by sharing roles and responsibilities between the actors for data production, management, processing and use in the water sector.

Some of the main domains requiring access to water-related data include:

- **sectoral water management** (e.g. drinking water supply, irrigation, energy, health and transportation)
- **integrated water sector planning** (e.g. local level, basin level, national level, transboundary basins, regional level)
- **climate change adaptation**
- **disaster risk reduction** (e.g. floods, water shortages, droughts)
- **reporting** (e.g. global, for SDGs; regional, for EU; national)
- **specific decision making** (e.g. operational management, territorial management, emergency situations)
- **other water sector activities** (e.g. regulatory aspects, public information).

The EUWI + project's work has supported implementation of integrated data management in applying the principles of the Shared Environmental Information System (Box 3.1). To this end, the EUWI+ project is supporting implementation of a platform and plan to facilitate automatic exchanges and integration of datasets produced and managed at the level of various institutions. It will do this through online "extract, transform, load" processes using new technologies (e.g. geographic web services and application programming interfaces).

> **Box 3.1. Principles of a Shared Environmental Information System (SEIS)**
>
> On 1 February 2008, the European Commission adopted a Communication on a Shared Environmental Information System (SEIS). It established SEIS to improve environmental data collection, exchange and use across Europe. At the 2011 UNECE Environment for Europe Conference in Nur-Sultan (then Astana), Kazakhstan, participating ministers agreed to develop SEIS across the broader pan-European region, including Eastern Partnership countries. According to their principles, information should be:
>
> - managed as close as possible to its source
> - collected once, and shared with others for many purposes
> - readily available to public authorities and enable them to easily fulfil their legal reporting obligations
> - readily accessible to end-users, primarily public authorities at all levels from local to European, to enable them to assess in a timely fashion the state of the environment and the effectiveness of their policies, and to design new policy
> - accessible to enable end-users, both public authorities and citizens, to make comparisons at the appropriate geographical scale (e.g. countries, cities, catchment areas) and to participate meaningfully in the development and implementation of environmental policy
> - fully available to the general public, after due consideration of the appropriate level of aggregation and subject to appropriate confidentiality constraints, and at national level in the relevant national language(s)
> - supported through common, free open standards.
>
> *Source:* European Environnment Agency (n.d.[8]), "Shared Enviromental Information System", https://www.eea.europa.eu/about-us/what/shared-environmental-information-system-1

3.2.1.2. Sound basin management in line with integrated water resources management principles

River basin management planning is a holistic and integrated approach to water resource management and aquatic ecosystems. It is used to improve human health and the quality of water resources and ecosystems, as well as foster economic development and consistency between sectoral policies. The output is a non-technical, clear planning document: the river basin management plan (RBMP). It is developed with an established methodology and public participation to enhance awareness and inform decision makers. The RBMP typically contains successive chapters describing characterisation of the river basin (drivers, pressures, status, impacts); diagnosis and main issues; trends and objectives; programme of measures and dashboard (see Box 3.2).

Box 3.2. Content and structure of river basin management plans

While the nature of river basin management plans differs from one situation to another, their structures have similarities.

FROM VISION TO STRATEGIC ACTION

River basin planning typically involves a series of nested statements of intent that together form the means for development and implementation. These relate to the basin vision and/or goal, more concrete objectives and specific actions. Vision statements are often aspirational rather than specific. They provide a preliminary indication of political purpose before difficult decisions over trade-offs and investment need to be made. Basin visions tend to be developed around one or more of the following priorities:

- Protection: Environmental state of the water resources in providing goods and services
- Development: Social and economic outcomes related to water use, land use or catchment areas
- Disaster risk: Human, property or ecological risks of flooding and other disasters
- Institutional: Institutional intent for co-operation, collaboration and stewardship

To be implemented, vision statements need to be translated into specific and measurable objectives and actions that are achievable with the available resources and given timeframe. The basin plan performs this function.

STAGES AND MILESTONES IN BASIN PLANNING

Basin planning typically considers a range of social, economic and environmental issues. However, the range of issues needs to be narrowed to key priorities to allow development of a high-level strategy. Based on these priorities and the strategy determined, detailed implementation planning is undertaken. This basin planning process can be represented in four key stages:

1. Conduct a situation assessment: Gain an understanding of the current and future conditions in the basin, as well as identify and prioritise key issues.
2. Formulate a vision and objectives: Spell out the desired state of the basin over the long term, together with goals (preliminary objectives) and principles to achieve this over time.
3. Develop basin strategies: Specify a coherent suite of strategic objectives and outcomes related to protection, use, disaster management and institutional development, designed to achieve the vision.
4. Detail implementation: Define actions that give effect to the basin strategies and should ultimately achieve the vision and objectives.

Initially, basin planning is narrow, identifying a limited number of key issues. It then broadens to detailed implementation planning. Central to the process is the identification of strategic priorities and trade-offs. These priorities are often developed via a wide stakeholder consultation. They are determined by social preferences about the economy, society and the environment. These choices are the fulcrum around which the basin planning process turns.

Source: Pegram et al. (2013[9]), *River Basin Planning: Principles, Procedures and Approaches for Strategic Basin Planning*, UNESCO, Paris, www.gwp.org/globalassets/global/toolbox/references/river-basin-planning.pdf

Geographical and methodological context

The Dnieper is the third longest river in Europe with a length of 2 201 km and a river basin area of 504 000 km². The Dnieper river basin is a cross-border system: 20% of its territory is in the Russian Federation, 23% in Belarus and 57% in Ukraine. Two sub-basins of the Dnieper river basin are in Belarus: Dnieper and Pripyat (Figure 3.2 and Table 3.4). The Pripyat river basin is transboundary as well, with 42% of its area in Belarus and 58% in Ukraine. The Pripyat river joins the Dnieper in Ukraine, in the Kyiv reservoir. These two basin districts (upper Dnieper and Pripyat) were selected for work under EUWI+ to develop and improve RBMPs. Following these experiences, Belarus improved its regulation concerning the content of future RBMPs.

Figure 3.2. Dnieper and Pripyat river basin districts in Belarus in the context of the wider Dnieper river basin

Source: ВИЕС+ (2019[10]), План управления бассейном реки Днепр [Dnieper River Basin Management Plan], РУП «Центральный научно-исследовательский институт комплексного использования водных ресурсов» (ЦНИИКИВР), Агентство по окружающей среде Австрии и Международный офис воды, www.cricuwr.by/plan_dnepr/

Table 3.4. Main characteristics of the upper Dnieper and Pripyat river basins

	upper Dnieper river basin	Pripyat river basin
Area (km²)	63 720	50 900
Population	5 million	1 million
Average flow (m³/s)	370	390

Source: EUWI+ (2019[10]), План управления бассейном реки Днепр [Dnieper River Basin Management Plan], Central Research Institute for Complex Use of Water Resources (CRICUWR), Umweltbundesamt and International Office for Water, www.cricuwr.by/plan_dnepr/; EUWI+ (2020[11]), План управления бассейном реки Припять (проект) [Pripyat River Basin Management Plan (draft)], Central Research Institute for Complex Use of Water Resources (CRICUWR), Umweltbundesamt and International Office for Water, http://www.cricuwr.by/plan_pr/

Dnieper RBMP

The Dnieper RBMP, which deals with the upper Dnieper basin located within the territory of Belarus, is the first one approved in Belarus. On 25 October 2018, during the first Belarus-Ukraine Forum, the second Dnieper Basin Council held in Gomel approved the Dnieper RBMP and launched the decentralised approval process. A Ukrainian delegation participated in the Basin Council, led by the deputy-president of State Agency for Water Resources of Ukraine, accompanied by the presidents of all four sub-basin authorities of Dnipro (downstream Dnieper) river basin. *Oblast*-level executive committees and the Minsk city executive committee approved the Dnieper RBMP on 31 December 2019.

A previous project funded by the European Union (EU), the Environmental Protection of International River Basins (EPIRB), had produced a draft of the Dnieper RBMP. The draft was further refined in the framework of EUWI+ through a new regulation concerning RBMP content published on 1 June 2017 that brought its content closer to WFD requirements.

Following these improvements, the validity period of the RBMP and implementation periods of the programme of measures were clarified. The improved plan took stock of human activities and pressures on the river basin, especially point and diffuse pollution sources. As a complementary output, a new guideline for estimating the pollution load from diffuse sources in Belarus drew on the experience of the Dnieper and Pripyat RBMPs.

The first implementation cycle of the Dnieper RBMP (2020-25) proposed 36 priority measures. It costs approximately EU 233 million, of which EUR 168 million (more than 70%) concerns the Minsk Wastewater Treatment Plan. This amount represents around 1% of the Dnieper basin's annual gross domestic product (GDP) and less than EUR 10 per inhabitant per year. For the second implementation cycle (2025-31), the additional 27 proposed measures (EUR 26 million) represent around 0.1% of the basin's annual GDP.

Pripyat RBMP

The Pripyat RBMP is closer to WFD requirements than the earlier Dnieper RBMP since it includes water bodies delineation and economic analysis, among other things. Furthermore, it expanded environmental objectives to SDGs.

The Pripyat RBMP development has delineated 636 river water bodies, 79 lakes and reservoirs and 11 groundwater bodies. Of these bodies, only 48 have relevant monitoring results. Overall, the quality of water in the basin's water bodies is classified as "good," but most have been heavily modified (see Section 2.3.3). The high ecological importance of Pripyat river basin (e.g. biodiversity, wetlands) is recognised through more than 6 000 km² of protected areas and the numerous areas designated under the Emerald Network.[2] To safeguard the basin's ecological wealth, the impacts of future projects must be rigorously and comprehensively studied. The Pripyat river basin abstracts 366 million m³ per year, 63% from surface water and 37% from groundwater.

Figure 3.3. Water abstractions from the Pripyat river basin by economic use

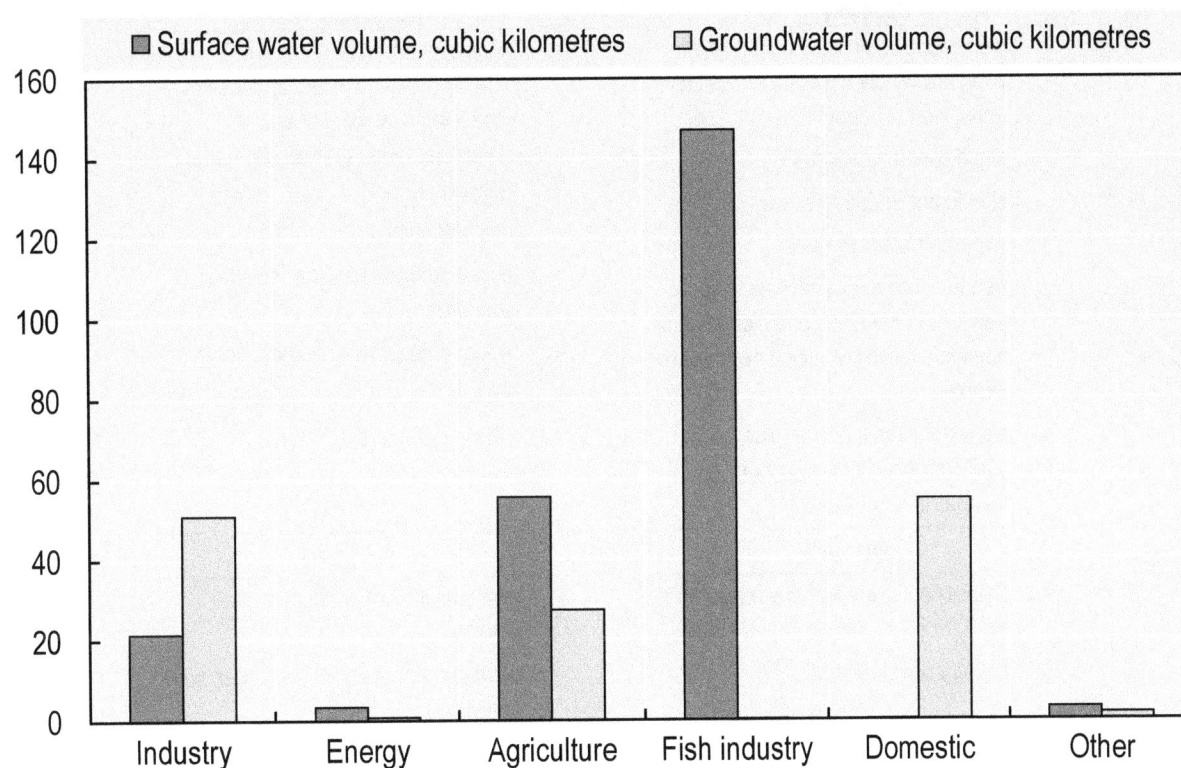

Source: CRICUWR (2019[12]), Водные ресурсы, их использование и качество вод (за 2018 год) [State Water Cadastre: Water Resources, their Use and Water Quality (in 2018)], Central Research Institute for Complex Use of Water Resources, Ministry of Natural Resources and Environmental Protection of the Republic of Belarus.

Table 3.5 briefly analyses strengths, weaknesses, opportunities and threats (SWOT) to summarise the river basin diagnostic.

Table 3.5. Pripyat RBMP: Brief SWOT analysis

Strengths	Weaknesses
• significant water resources (water uses are widely covered, as well as ecosystems' needs) • significant forest areas • significant wetlands areas • mineral resources • nearly full coverage of water supply services in the cities and high level of service availability, including for poor people • significant sanitation service availability in cities with good standards of purification.	• significant anthropogenic modifications of hydrographic system and loss of ecosystems' functions after melioration and other engineering activities • lack of funding • lack of centralised water supply in rural area • lack of data (water-related diseases, etc.).
Opportunities	**Threats**
• Belarusian regulation to strengthen legal scope of RBMP, Water Code • country development.	• intensification of agriculture and industry • development of economic zones with specific rules • impacts of the Chernobyl disaster • climate change.

Source: EUWI+ (2020[11]), План управления бассейном реки Припять (проект) [Pripyat River Basin Management Plan (draft)], Central Research Institute for Complex Use of Water Resources (CRICUWR), Umweltbundesamt and International Office for Water, http://www.cricuwr.by/plan_pr/

The Pripyat RBMP's programme of measures will be implemented during 2021-30 for an estimated cost of EUR 456 million. This amount includes EUR 101 million for climate change adaptation, leaving EUR 355 million to improve surface bodies. Figure 3.4 shows the proposed budget breakdown. A major challenge is to organise the funding mechanisms and the financing between the national and *oblast*-level budgets from national and foreign sources, both public and private.

Figure 3.4. Pripyat programme of measures 2021-30: Proposed breakdown of costs

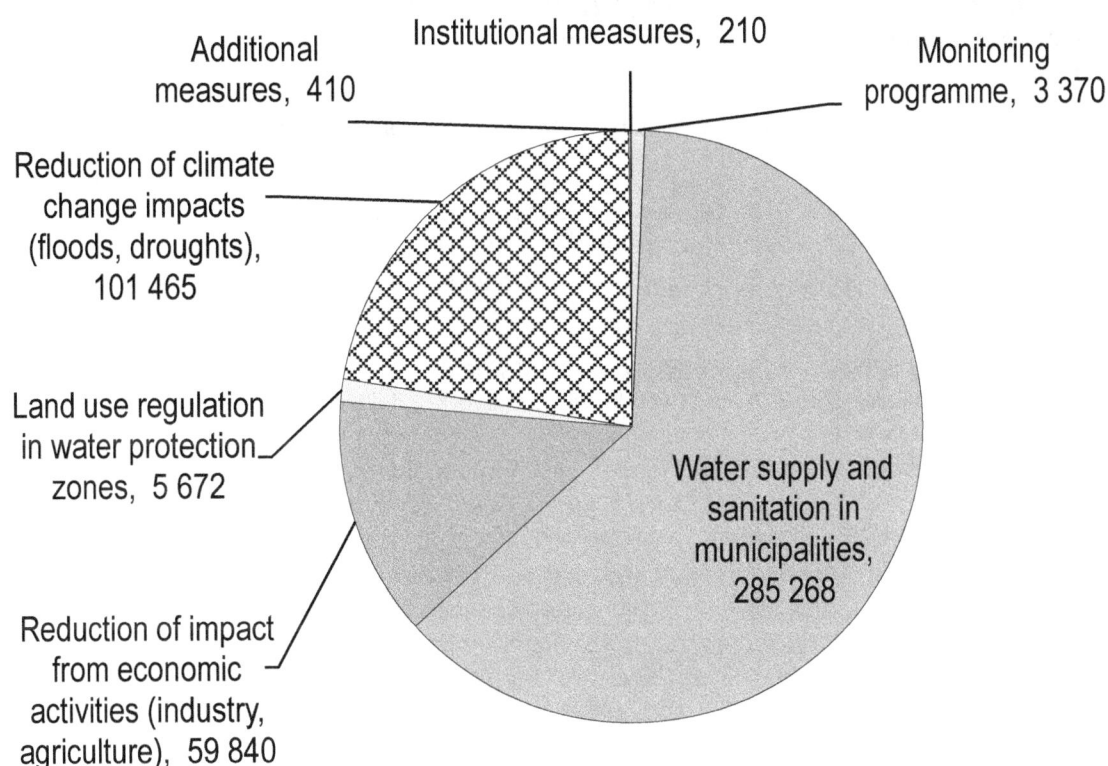

Additional measures, 410 — Institutional measures, 210 — Monitoring programme, 3 370

Reduction of climate change impacts (floods, droughts), 101 465

Land use regulation in water protection zones, 5 672

Reduction of impact from economic activities (industry, agriculture), 59 840

Water supply and sanitation in municipalities, 285 268

Source: EUWI+ (2020[11]), План управления бассейном реки Припять (проект) [Pripyat River Basin Management Plan (draft)], Central Research Institute for Complex Use of Water Resources (CRICUWR), Umweltbundesamt and International Office for Water, http://www.cricuwr.by/plan_pr/

The Pripyat RBMP initiated a consultation process. Non-governmental organisations (NGOs) and local stakeholders have taken part in two meetings in Minsk and Gomel *oblasts*. The comments received helped experts improve the draft RBMP.

In 2014, the new Water Code of the Republic of Belarus established the procedure for creating basin councils and outlined the main requirements for developing RBMPs. By law, development of RBMPs for the five largest river basins was envisaged: for the Dnieper, Daugava/West Dvina, West Bug, Neman and Pripyat basins. In 2016-18, three basin councils were created (Dnieper, West Bug and Pripyat). Their members are representatives of local executive bodies from administrative units located in the basin, as well as several ministries (the Ministry of Natural Resources and Environmental Protection, the Ministry of Housing and Communal Services, the Ministry of Transport) and representatives of major water users, academia and civil society organisations. The draft Water Strategy 2030 foresaw the creation of two more river basin management councils for the Neman basin (by 2022) and the West Dvina/Daugava basin (by 2024) (Minprirody, 2018[3]).

3.2.1.3. Protocol on Water and Health

UNECE and the World Health Organization Regional Office for Europe jointly service the Protocol on Water and Health. Belarus, which has been a Party to the Protocol since 2009, considers it a key instrument for international co-operation in the area of water and sanitation. Global objectives of the Protocol are to be achieved by establishing national and local target indicators under each main area covered by the Protocol (20 areas in total), along with target dates and measures required to achieve the targets. Thanks to its effective target setting and reporting mechanism well tested over the past 15 years, the Protocol is being promoted in Europe as an effective tool for achieving the SDGs on water, sanitation and water resources protection. Parties to the Protocol have the obligation to monitor progress towards the set targets and revise targets once achieved. They must also report on their implementation at the national and international level.

In November 2019, Belarus was elected as the Chair of the Bureau of the Meeting of the Parties to the Protocol.

Belarus adopted its first set of national targets and measures to achieve them in 2013. Five years later, it launched the National Policy Dialogues process under EUWI+. The country identified revision of the Protocol targets on water and sanitation in line with key regional and global policies as a priority area for support.

Following endorsement by the EUWI+ Inter-agency Steering Committee, the process started in December 2018 with a baseline analysis. This looked at the legal framework, environment and health, institutional and financial arrangements and public participation aspects. In so doing, it sought to identify priorities and needs for action and recommend establishing targets in the Protocol target-setting areas (art. 6.2 of the Protocol). This inter-sectoral analysis was carried out by the Ministry of Health, Ministry of Natural Resources and Environmental Protection, Ministry of Housing and Communal Services, other professionals, NGO representatives and international experts. It set the basis for 27 new targets covering 17 target areas of the Protocol. The Steering Committee discussed the draft targets and action with the measures to achieve them on several occasions. An internal inter-ministerial consultation involved the above authorities, as well as the Ministry of Education, the Ministry of Emergency Situations and the National Statistics Committee (*Belstat*). The final set of targets (available in Russian and English) was expected to be adopted through a joint decree by the Ministry of Health and Ministry of Natural Resources and Environment Protection in June 2020.

The new targets set with support of EUWI+ are aligned with the objectives and principles of the SDGs. They also reflect the EU policy goals related to prevention, safety, risk-based approaches, equity of access and attention to hygiene in institutional settings.

3.2.1.4 Local capacity development

EUWI+ has supported Belarusian experts through capacity building in the form of technical meetings, workshops, trainings, field surveys, videoconferences and training materials. Beyond RBMP development and strengthened skills, outputs include guidelines concerning diffuse sources pollution, RBMP delineation and monitoring, which can feed into secondary legislation.

3.2.2. Support at sectoral, regional and basin levels

3.2.2.1. Developing water supply and sanitation in rural settings

As was already mentioned in section 2.2.4 above, the Kopyl *rayon* in Belarus's central Minsk *oblast* is predominantly rural. Due in part to its low population density, the *rayon* is peculiar for the involvement of non-traditional operators in its centralised water supply services. Of Kopyl *rayon*'s 208 settlements, only 56 have access to centralised piped water supply. Of these 56, only 26 receive their water supply exclusively from Kopyl Housing and Municipal Utilities (*Копыльское ЖКХ*), a communal unitary enterprise established to provide such services. Agricultural firms supply water to 27 rural settlements (4 of which are also connected to the utility company's services). State education facilities provide water to four settlements (three in conjunction with the utility company, and one together with agricultural firms). Half of the 208 settlements in Kopyl *rayon* have no more than 30 residents and 58 have no more than 10. With such low population sizes, it is not economically viable to provide centralised drinking water supply (CRICUWR, 2019[13]).

Unlike Kopyl Housing and Public Utilities which supplies water as part of its business model, agricultural firms and education facilities supply water informally to local residents. Since the service is free and without contracts, there is no cost recovery. These firms and facilities also lack qualified experts. Consequently, the water supply does not benefit from oversight to ensure its suitability for human consumption, reliability of service or speed of flow. Legislation has been adopted to resolve this problem, but secondary legislation and implementation are lacking (CRICUWR, 2019[13]).

Recommendations for a future master plan on potable water supply in Koply *rayon* were developed with support from EUWI+ to address the challenge of potable water supply in rural settlements (Section 2.2.4 for more information on these challenges).

3.2.2.2. Support to improving water-use efficiency in the most water-intensive industries and protecting water resources from their activities: the case of the three most water-intensive enterprises in Kopyl district

The status of water resources is assessed through monitoring and data. Subsequently, measures should be based on the assigned status of water bodies. To further improve water management, water use and wastewater discharge norms are described in the examples below about the most four water-intensive enterprises in Kopyl *rayon*:

- Kopyl Housing and Public Utilities (*Копыльское ЖКХ*), a communal unitary enterprise
- the Kopyl branch of the Slutsk Cheese Factory (*ОАО Слуцкий сыродельный комбинат*), an open joint-stock company
- "Kopylskoye" (*ОАО «Копыльское»*) and Staritsa-Agro (*ОАО «Старица-Агро»*), agricultural open joint-stock companies that raise livestock, produce milk and cultivate crops.

These four firms were selected following an evaluation of water resources in Kopyl *rayon* and a resulting list of 27 water users because they alone accounted for 64% of water abstractions in Kopyl *rayon* in 2016 (CRICUWR, 2018[14]).

Kopyl has underdeveloped wastewater infrastructure. The main sinks for wastewater flows in the district are bodies of water, infiltration fields, earthen storage pits and cesspools. The vast majority (81.1% of wastewater) discharges directly into the environment (CRICUWR, 2018[14]).

In accordance with the Water Code, firms must develop and implement "technological" standards of water use and wastewater disposal. Water use by enterprises falls into three categories: for use directly in production; for use indirectly in the production process; and use for household and drinking water needs. EUWI+ analysed Kopyl *rayon*'s four largest water users and calculated normative volumes of water use for each one to help optimise water use.

For the Slutsk Cheese Factory, for example, EUWI+ calculated technological norms for water use and wastewater discharge to produce a tonne of milk. This allows the firm to plan its activities and calculate its water-use volumes. Further analysis compared the company's production techniques to the industry's best available techniques. It then designed measures to improve freshwater savings and reduce pollution released in wastewater by modernising local purification facilities. This reduces the burden on Kopyl city's facilities and, as a result, on the Mazha river into which wastewaters from Kopyl town are finally discharged (CRICUWR, 2018[14]).

For Staritsa-Agro and Kopylskoe, EUWI+ established balances of water usage and discharge for each plot of land with centralised water supply and sanitation. These show the maximum volume of water the firm can extract in each plot under current conditions of water use. Exceeding this volume would qualify as irrational water use. As part of this work, recommendations were provided on water accounting, the use of artesian wells, and the preservation and rational use of water resources (CRICUWR, 2018[14]).

Kopyl Housing and Public Utilities is tasked with the provision of quality drinking water to population and firms. EUWI+ calculated the normative losses and unaccounted-for water consumption from systems of water supply, as well as norms for technological water consumption. The standard losses and unaccounted-for water consumption in general for the city of Kopyl and other settlements in Kopyl *rayon* amounted to 47.18% (38.56% in Kopyl city, 63.85% in other settlements) (CRICUWR, 2018[14]).

These high figures are largely due to the age and composition of the distribution network. Most of the water supply networks in Kopyl *rayon* are old (69% are at least 20-years-old), particularly in the city of Kopyl (86% of its network is at least 20-years-old), making them susceptible to leaks (Figure 3.5). Another contributing factor to the high loss rates through leakage is the prevalence of cast iron pipes. These pipes have twice the standard leak rate (2.4 litre/minute per km) as steel pipes (1.2 litre/minute per km). The leak rate is much higher than with polyethylene pipes. In all, 79.1% of Kopyl city's pipes are cast iron, while polyethylene (18.65%) and steel (2.25%) make up the remainder. In other settlements, cast iron (47.22%) and polyethylene (46.34%) are nearly equally common, with steel accounting for the remaining 6.44% (CRICUWR, 2019[13]). The phased replacement of deteriorated parts/segments of the Kopyl *rayon*'s water distribution network could help reduce loss rates and increase efficiency of water use.

Figure 3.5. Age of water supply piping in Kopyl *rayon*

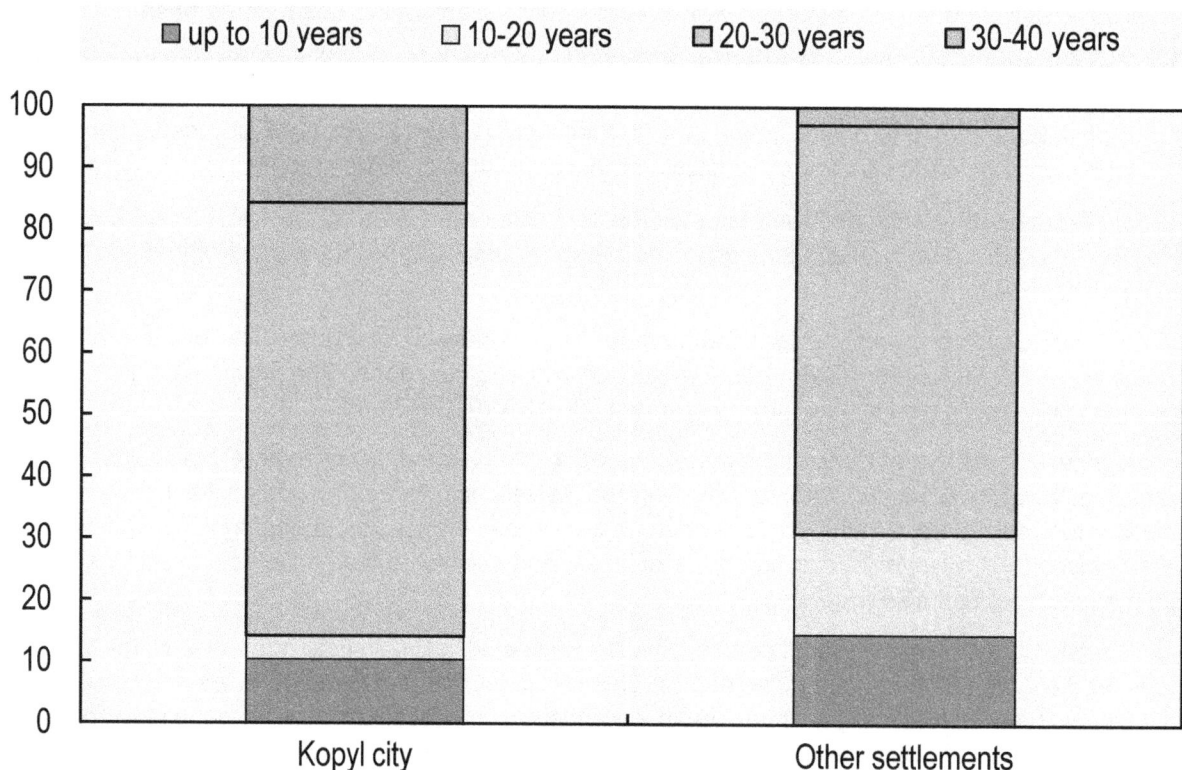

Source: CRICUWR (2018[14]), «Об оценке эффективности использования воды и разработке новых технологических нормативов потребления воды и сброса сточных вод для самых водоемких предприятий Копыльского района Минской области Беларуси» [On Evaluating the Effectiveness of Water Use and the Development of New Technological Norms for Water Use and Discharge of Wastewater for the Most Water-intensive Firms in the Kopyl *Rayon* of the Minsk *Oblast* of Belarus], prepared by a team of experts led by P. Zakharko from the Central Research Institute for Complex Use of Water Resources, Ministry of Natural Resources and Environmental Protection of the Republic of Belarus.

3.2.2.3. Rehabilitating irrigation infrastructure: a pilot study in Gomel oblast

Redundant infrastructure may have potential to increase strategic storage of water at times of plenty and support water demand in low flow periods during growing seasons. Given its seasonal water shortages and the significance of agriculture to the local economy, Gomel *oblast* was identified as a pilot region that might benefit from the rehabilitation of irrigation infrastructure. This exercise would aim to support water security objectives and increase agricultural productivity. In 2020, EUWI+ supported an assessment of the economic feasibility and water security impacts and trade-offs of rehabilitating or adapting the region's irrigation infrastructure. In parallel, discussions on changing land use for agricultural and general purposes in response to the impact of changing climate conditions on water resources will inform the policy debate.

3.2.2.4. Sub-basin management plans

EUWI+ developed sub-basin management plans to solve local issues identified during Dnieper RBMP refinement (Section 3.2.1.2). A sub-basin management plan is a tool to implement a programme of measures. This activity is organised at a hydrographic scale closer to the field and local issues. It is consistent with the RBMP as a nested process. EUWI+ supported the development of two sub-basin management plans i/n Dnieper river basin; in the Uza river basin; and for the urban watercourses in the town of Mogilev to improve their ecological status.

A sub-basin management plan includes the characterisation of the sub-basins through specific monitoring, field surveys (in accordance with EUWI+ trainings), census, diagnosis, objectives, programme of measures with costs and planning, and results of consultations with local stakeholders.

1) Uza river basin

Uza is a small river in Gomel *oblast* and a tributary of Sozh river. The length of the river is 76 km and its catchment area is 944 km². Uza sub-basin is in the territory of Gomel, Buda-Koshelevo and Vetka *rayon*s (administrative districts). The hydrographic network of Uza river contains the following watercourses: Zhurbitsa, Khochemlya, Belichanka, Ivolka and Randovka rivers; Rogovskoi, Milchanskiyi and Krasnaya canals; and a number of drainage canals. The river valley of Uza river has a width from 600-800 m; the width of the river channel is only 5-8 m upstream. Up to 15 m downstream, annual discharge in the mouth is 3.4 m³/s.

In recent years, the ecological status of the Uza river and its downstream tributaries has been classified as "bad" (4th class). The main reason for this classification is the substantial impact of Gomel, the second largest city in the country, on the watershed area, the watercourse and its tributaries. Many local industries including Gomelvodokanal (a water utility) discharge significant amounts of wastewater, while the city's territory is a large source of diffuse pollution (e.g. transported by storm waters).

Therefore, Uza river is considered as one of the most polluted in the upper Dnieper river basin, as well as in Belarus.. As Uza river flows into the transboundary Sozh river, restoration and enhancement of ecological status of Uza river and its tributaries is a priority for Dnieper RBMP implementation in Belarus.

2) Urban watercourses in Mogilev

In recent decades, with rainfall intensification during the summer, Mogilev – the third largest city of Belarus after Minsk and Gomel - has regularly experienced submergence. When developing a rainwater collection network for new facilities, designers do not organise a separate release of surface wastewater into a water body. Instead, they seek to connect to the existing rainwater drainage network to avoid the need to build wastewater treatment plants. In the situation of active new housing construction in the city and reducing the size of watershed area with permeable subsoil, this practice aggravates the submergence problems.

There are a number of small water courses in the city of Mogilev: Dubrovenka river with its tributaries Strushnya and Kazimirovsky streams; and Debrya river. They receive significant discharges of untreated surface wastewater from the city (there are more than 60 outfalls of rainwater sewers). Both the volumes and quality of the discharges impact the environmental status of the river segment located within the city's territory.

The ecological status of Debrya stream was assessed in 2016/17 as "very bad". The environmental status of the aforementioned watercourses and the state of the rain drainage network in the catchments of small watercourses of Mogilev should be assessed, and main sources of water pollution identified. Key challenges related to the rainwater sewage network in the city and a set of measures to reduce the impact on watercourses should be identified. This work will help achieve a greater level of protection of small watercourses in Mogilev and then reduce the anthropogenic effects on the Dnieper river.

As of September 2020, sub-basin management plans were still in development.

3.2.2.5. Transboundary co-operation

Belarus attaches considerable importance to enhancing transboundary water co-operation with neighbouring states. Within the country workplan of Belarus under the EUWI+, UNECE facilitated activities on transboundary water co-operation with Latvia and Lithuania.

In January 2018, with the support of the EUWI+ project, Belarus and Latvia delegations met to prepare an agreement on the protection and use of transboundary waters in the West Dvina/Daugava basin. The two countries considered further options in later communication. Belarus and Latvia were expected to sign an inter-agency agreement on the transboundary West Dvina/Daugava basin by the end of 2020.

Under EUWI+, with support of the EU, UNECE also facilitated the continuation of technical co-operation between Belarus and Lithuania in the Neman river basin. The Belarus-Lithuania expert group on enhancing bilateral co-operation in the Neman river basin held a third meeting in Minsk on 15 May 2018. It involved the Ministry of Natural Resources and Environmental Protection of Belarus, Ministry of Environment of Lithuania and other concerned stakeholders. The meeting completed the final report of the second phase of the elaboration of the priority components of the joint RBMP for the Neman basin to enhance transboundary co-operation. The findings and data of the report, in turn, laid a solid foundation for completion of a joint RBMP for the Neman basin. This could happen within an upcoming Global Environment Facility project, expected to start by the end of 2020.

In another important achievement, Belarus signed an intergovernmental agreement on transboundary water protection with Poland on 7 February 2020. Once ratified by both Parties, the agreement foresees the establishment of a joint body, which will oversee implementation.

Notes

[1] Sustainable Development Goals, the Paris Agreement, the Water Convention, the Protocol on Water and Health (in support of implementation and monitoring of SDG 6.1, 6.2, 6.3 and 3.9), Espoo Convention, the SEA Protocol, EU directives on strategic environmental assessment and environmental impact assessment, and relevant bilateral agreements on transboundary water bodies.

[2] The Emerald Network of Areas of Special Conservation Interest is a set of protected nature sites established through the Council of Europe's Bern Convention to conserve biodiversity. For more information, see www.coe.int/en/web/bern-convention/emerald-network.

References

Belstat (2019), *С.14. Население, обеспеченное очисткой сточных вод [С. 14. Population Connected to Wastewater Treatment]*, (database), https://www.belstat.gov.by/ofitsialnaya-statistika/makroekonomika-i-okruzhayushchaya-sreda/okruzhayuschaya-sreda/sovmestnaya-sistema-ekologicheskoi-informatsii2/c-vodnye-resursy/s-14-naselenie-obespechennoe-ochistkoi-stochnyh-vod/   [6]

Belstat (2019), *С.5. Вода, поставляемая отраслью водоснабжения, и доступ населения к этой воде [С.5. Water Provided by the Water Supply Industry and Access of the Population to that Water]*, (database), https://www.belstat.gov.by/ofitsialnaya-statistika/makroekonomika-i-okruzhayushchaya-sreda/okruzhayuschaya-sreda/sovmestnaya-sistema-ekologicheskoi-informatsii2/c-vodnye-resursy/s-5-voda-postavlyaemaya-otraslyu-vodosnabzheniya-i-dostup-naseleniya-k-etoi-v   [4]

Belstat (2019), *С.6. Доступ населения к централизованному водоснабжению [С.6. Access of the Population to Centralised Water Supply]*, (database), https://www.belstat.gov.by/ofitsialnaya-statistika/makroekonomika-i-okruzhayushchaya-sreda/okruzhayuschaya-sreda/sovmestnaya-sistema-ekologicheskoi-informatsii2/c-vodnye-resursy/s-6-dostup-naseleniya-k-tsentralizovannomu-vodosnabzheniyu/   [5]

CRICUWR (2019), *Государственный водный кадастр: Водные ресурсы, их использование и качество вод (за 2018 год) [State Water Cadastre: Water Resources, Their Use and Water Quality (in 2018)]*, Central Research Institute for Complex Use of Water Resources, Ministry of Natural Resources and Environmental Protection of the Republic of Belarus, Minsk.   [12]

CRICUWR (2019), *Разработка рекомендаций по развитию систем хозяйственно-питьевого водоснабжения в Копыльском районе Минской области Беларуси [Elaboration of Recommendations on the Development of Domestic Drinking Water Supply]*, Central Research Institute for Complex Use of Water Resources, Ministry of Natural Resources and Environmental Protection of the Republic of Belarus, Minsk.   [13]

CRICUWR (2018), *Об оценке эффективности использования воды и разработке новых технологических нормативов потребления воды и сброса сточных вод для самых водоемких предприятий Копыльского района Минской области Беларуси [On Evaluating the Effectiveness of Water Use and the Development of New Technological Norms for Water Use and Discharge of Wastewater for the Most Water-intensive Firms in the Kopyl District of the Minsk Region of Belarus]*, Central Research Institute for Complex Use of Water Resources, Ministry of Natural Resources and Environmental Protection of the Republic of Belarus, Minsk.   [14]

CRICUWR (2018), *Помощь правительству Беларуси в национализации индикаторов для мониторинга прогресса в реализации SDG 6.3 – 6.5 [Assistance to the Government of Belarus in the Nationalisation of Indicators for the Monitoring of Progress Towards Achieving SDG 6.3-6.5]*, Dubianok, S (ed.), Central Research Institute for Complex Use of Water Resources, Ministry of Natural Resources and Environmental Protection of the Republic of Belarus, Minsk.   [7]

CRICUWR (2018), *Стратегия управления водными ресурсами в условиях изменения климата на период до 2030 года (проект) [The Strategy of Water Resource Management with the Account of Climate Change Adaptation for the Period Until 2030: Draft]*, Central Research Institute for Complex Use of Water Resources, Ministry of Natural Resources and Environmental Protection of the Republic of Belarus, Minsk.   [2]

European Environment Agency (n.d.), *Shared Environmental Information System (SEIS)*, https://www.eea.europa.eu/about-us/what/shared-environmental-information-system-1 (accessed on 10 July 2020).   [8]

EUWI+ (2020), *План управления бассейном реки Припять (проект) [Pripyat River Basin Management Plan (draft)]*, Central Research Institute for Complex Use of Water Resources (CRICUWR), Umweltbundesamt and International Office for Water, http://www.cricuwr.by/plan_pr/ (accessed on 29 July 2020).   [11]

EUWI+ (2019), *План управления бассейном реки Днепр*, Central Research Institute for Complex Use of Water Resources (CRICUWR), Umweltbundesamt and International Office for Water, http://www.cricuwr.by/plan_dnepr/.   [10]

EUWI+ (2018), *Infographics: River Basin Management Plan (Инфографики: план управления речными бассейнами)*, https://www.euwipluseast.eu/en/component/k2/item/430-infographics-river-basin-management-plan-en?fromsearch=1 (accessed on 10 августа 2020 г.).   [15]

Minprirody (2018), *Стратегия управления водными ресурсами в условиях изменения климата на период до 2030 года (проект) [The Strategy of Water Resource Management in the Context of Climate Change Adaptation for the Period Until 2030: Draft]*, Central Research Institute for Complex Use of Water Resources, Ministry of Natural Resources and Environmental Protection of the Republic of Belarus, Minsk.   [3]

Pegram, G. et al. (2013), *River Basin Planning: Principles, Procedures and Approaches for Strategic Basin Planning*, UNESCO, Paris, https://www.gwp.org/globalassets/global/toolbox/references/river-basin-planning.pdf.   [9]

Strelkovskii, N. et al. (2019), *Navigating through Deep Waters of Uncertainty: Systems Analysis Approach to Strategic Planning of Water Resources and Water Infrastructure under High Uncertainties and Conflicting Interests*, International Institute for Applied Systems Analysis, Laxenburg, Austria and OECD Publishing, Paris.   [1]

4 Next steps

This chapter assesses opportunities to boost water security in Belarus by supporting the country's ongoing reform agenda. It summarises the successes that Belarus has achieved, such as progress on harmonising its water policy with the EU's Water Framework Directive and integrated water resources management principles as well as the development of river basin management plans for two of Belarus's transboundary river basins. It also highlights improvements in Belarus's inter-ministerial co-ordination on water management, efforts to achieve the water-related Sustainable Development Goals (SDGs) and international co-operation on transboundary watercourses and lakes. The chapter concludes with a list of potential areas for further work to improve water security in Belarus.

4.1. The Belarus water policy reform journey has yielded early success stories

The Republic of Belarus (hereafter "Belarus") worked with implementing partners on the European Union Water Initiative Plus for the Eastern Partnership (EUWI+) project. It made significant progress towards an ambitious country programme that could drive improvements in its water policy framework. This is the first time that Belarus and the EUWI has engaged over a sustained period of time.

While Belarus has no formal legal obligations to align its laws to the EU's water *acquis*, it has recognised the benefits of aligning with key principles such as the Water Framework Directive (WFD). To that end, Belarus has embraced requirements of international obligations and linked it to its water policy reform agenda, securing synergies and driving implementation. For example, it has enshrined key features in the water-related Sustainable Development Goals (SDGs) in its draft Strategy of Water Resource Management in the Context of Climate Change for the Period until 2030 (hereafter "Water Strategy 2030").

Since 2016, Belarus has made progress with the development, consultation and launch of its new water strategy. It has also moved towards development and implementation of river basin management plans (RBMPs) for the Dnieper and Pripyat basins, and its progression of commitments under the water-related SDGs and Protocol on Water and Health.

This progress has been supported by data generated through significant efforts in monitoring and analysis of groundwater and surface water in line with WFD requirements. Indeed, stakeholder consultation and public participation have been key features of developing RBMPs. They have helped make water policy reform more inclusive and balance the interests and needs of a wide range of interested parties and water users.

Belarus has also increased inter-ministerial dialogue by creating the national "Inter-Agency Committee Managing the EUWI+ Implementation in Belarus". This platform is chaired by the deputy minister of the Ministry of Natural Resources and Environmental Protection (Minprirody). Other participating ministries have included the Ministry of Foreign Affairs, Ministry of Housing and Communal Services, Ministry of Health, Ministry of Agriculture and Food Stuffs and Ministry of Economy, *Belstat* and representatives of organisations and territorial bodies subordinated to Minprirody. The platform has involved operators including Belvodokanal and also participation from academia, including the Belarusian State Technical University.

The platform has allowed inter-ministerial discussion of national-level priorities, including consultation on the development of Water Strategy 2030. It has also considered reporting against international obligations, including the progress achieved in co-operation with neighbouring countries (Russian Federation, Ukraine, EU member states) in the field of transboundary water management. While at an early stage, progress and participation have been promising. This platform may mature into an established National Policy Dialogue similar to those operational in other Eastern Partnership countries.

Water security has been at the heart of the national work programme under EUWI+. Pilot actions in Kopyl *rayon* (district) have focused on such issues as rural water supply, water quality and water efficiency. They have delivered recommendations that will influence water supply and consumption in Belarus for generations to come.

The recommendations on developing potable water supply will contribute to achieving SDG 6.1 in the pilot rayon. While by analysing the water consumption norms of the water-intensive industries in the *rayon*, EUWI+ has helped Belarus identify inefficiencies that have been "baked in" to the design process for many years. This will help inform future planning and forecasting exercises. Encouraging industries to be more water-efficient has a knock-on effect. It reduces the production of wastewater, preserving the environment from the impact of potential discharges. This project to review design norms has potential for replication throughout Belarus. Implementation should be monitored.

This work has highlighted the regional variation in water availability in Belarus. It has also demonstrated that water-intensive activities, notably agricultural activities, are often in areas with seasonal water shortages and high sensitivity to climate change. The irrigation study in Gomel *oblast* (region) aimed to estimate the wider economic benefits of rehabilitating legacy infrastructure to take advantage of seasonal shifts in water availability. Collecting water during peak times of availability and storing it for use in irrigation at times of lower water availability may offer wider economic benefits to the agricultural regions in the southern parts of Belarus. This study was ongoing at the time of drafting this report.

The co-operation with Belarus has also focused on capacity development and coaching the environmentalists, water specialists and economists of the future. Training materials, for example, were developed on the use of economic instruments for managing water resources and bodies, and water systems. These materials have been prepared for pilot testing at two universities in Belarus during the winter term of 2020.

4.2. The reform journey is long and opportunities for follow-up activities have been uncovered

The EUWI+ project is scheduled to complete its activities in Belarus in 2021, but the water reform journey will continue. While the country has made progress, the process has exposed outstanding issues. Proposed future actions are highlighted below.

4.2.1. Support implementation of Water Strategy 2030

With regards to national-level policy reforms, future work in Belarus should consider supporting implementation of Water Strategy 2030. This would necessarily include actions at the basin and local levels. Existing economic instruments and subsidies should be improved, for example, and new instruments introduced for water resources management. This might include discharge fees based on pollutant load.

4.2.2. Identify and implement ways to ensure equitable access to water supply and sanitation

Work in Belarus should identify and implement measures for facilitating equitable access to water supply and sanitation (WSS). Such work should include support to amendments of related legal acts and priority investments in WSS. The National Policy Dialogue and an expanded version of the existing inter-agency co-operation platform would oversee this work. It should build capacity of local stakeholders in areas such as the use of economic analysis and instruments.

4.2.3. Work towards meeting international obligations

To progress towards meeting its international obligations, Belarus should act in three areas. First, it should further support transboundary water co-operation (e.g. on West Dvina) and reporting under the UN's Water Convention. Second, it should make progress in monitoring and reporting on water-related SDGs (SDG 6, SDG 3). Finally, it should support implementation of the revised targets under the Protocol on Water and Health.

4.2.4. Move forward on river basin management plans

Belarus should move forward on its river basin management plans (RBMPs) based on their state of evolution:

- Formally approve the Pripyat RBMP and commence implementation of selected measures.
- Pursue follow-up work on the Dnieper RBMP to ensure delineation of water bodies is closer to WFD requirements and begin preparing the second RBM planning cycle. Consider further selected measures under the Dnieper plan.
- Assess consistency between the final Dnipro RBMP (Ukraine) and Dnieper and Pripyat RBMPs in Belarus given the transboundary nature of the country's key rivers.
- Develop RBMP for the West Dvina and Neman river basins, mainstreaming these principles in the broader policy context in Belarus. In this way, development of relevant technical secondary legislation would help strengthen the alignment of RBMPs with WFD requirements.
- Support implementation of the EU's Nitrates Directive in Belarus given the impact of agriculture on water management. Capacity building should target basin management at central and *oblast* level and at the basin scale. Belarus should support the functioning of basin councils, and aim to improve consultation and stakeholder involvement process.
- Continue to collect and use high-quality data, which has been key to develop evidence-based policy and decision making under EUWI+. This would include the following:
  - moving towards a national master plan for data production and management
  - reinforcing national water databases
  - developing interoperability between information systems
  - reinforcing data processing and information production for decision making
  - facilitating public access to water data.

- Ensure the highest quality of data is gathered under the proposed management system. Capacity building in surface water and groundwater monitoring should consider new biological and chemical quality elements. It should also improve and target monitoring systems for specific sites, parameters and data. Selected government laboratories should complete training in laboratory methods and deepen technical competence.

4.2.5. Other possible future activities include the following:

- Support implementation of Water Strategy 2030 and of the future national WSS Strategy.
- Explore synergies between technical work and political decisions with regard to objectives of the programmes of measures under the RBMPs. Such work would identify good practices that can inspire further progress in Belarus and other Eastern Partnership countries. It could also provide policy and methodological guidance for better recovery of the costs of good water management.
- Provide further support to expand the frequency, capacity, quality and geographic and technical scope of biological, hydromorphological and chemical monitoring of surface waters. This would be in line with WFD practices, as well as with the strategic guidance on monitoring and assessment of transboundary waters under the Water Convention. Crucial follow-up is needed in the (re)accreditation and quality management of reference laboratories. Similar support should be provided for groundwater, including strengthening chemical and quantitative monitoring, its protection and sustainable use.
- Expand work on developing, adopting and implementing the approved RBMPs to other river basin districts. This includes sharing experiences around methodology e.g. through secondary legislation. It should also support institutional reform, expand dissemination of lessons learned in the six countries; and initiate implementation.

- Pursue establishment of basin councils and guide their work, including development and presentation of the business case for their sustainable financial operation. This would facilitate RBMP implementation and strengthen decentralisation of water management.

- Support harmonisation and strategic prioritisation of parameters and indicators, and the adoption of strategic data management, with open access and exchange between stakeholders, feeding into sound data analysis. This would ensure that improved data, collected through enhanced monitoring infrastructure, are appropriately shared and inform decisions.

- Continue to build capacity and raise awareness among stakeholders in the water sector. This would include increasing competences and involvement in pilot river basin councils. It would address water users' awareness on behavioural impacts on the water balance within each basin. And it would promote regional exchange of good practices in sustainable water use. Work with universities and academic institutions should continue, with water management, monitoring and biological assessment systems established in the curricula. This long-term capacity building would provide the national environmental institutions and the private sector with better-educated staff with relevant water management competences.

www.ingramcontent.com/pod-product-compliance
Lightning Source LLC
Chambersburg PA
CBHW081513200326
41518CB00015B/2481